To my lit   t"
   Enjoy
Know you will - you've
been on about it
for long enough!!!

       Love,
        Cheeky X

SUNLIT WATERS

SUNLIT WATERS

SUNLIT WATERS

AN INTRODUCTION TO THE ART OF FISHING WITH LIGHT TACKLE

By

CAPT. C. W. W. S. CONWAY
Indian Army

NATRAJ PUBLISHERS
DEHRA DUN

FIRST PUBLISHED APRIL 1942
FIRST INDIAN EDITION 1999

ISBN 81-85019-85-1

*Published by Mrs. Veena Arora for Natraj Publishers, Publications
Division, Dehra Dun and printed at Jaysons Quadra Colour Printers,
New Delhi*

꙰꙰꙰꙰꙰꙰꙰꙰꙰꙰꙰꙰꙰꙰꙰꙰꙰꙰꙰꙰꙰꙰꙰꙰꙰꙰

THIS BOOK IS DEDICATED

TO

BUNNY

WHO IN SPITE OF NOT FISHING HERSELF

AND IN SPITE OF LEAVE SPENT IN UNCOMFORTABLE PLACES

AND UNDER VERY TRYING CONDITIONS

STILL ENCOURAGES ME TO FISH.

MY GRATITUDE CANNOT BE ADEQUATELY EXPRESSED IN WORDS.

꙰꙰꙰꙰꙰꙰꙰꙰꙰꙰꙰꙰꙰꙰꙰꙰꙰꙰꙰꙰꙰꙰꙰꙰꙰꙰

❊❊❊❊❊❊❊❊❊❊❊❊❊❊❊❊❊❊❊❊❊❊❊❊❊❊❊❊❊❊❊❊❊❊

PREFACE

*P*REFACES are not made upon oath and therefore apologies are worthless. Criticism is easy, and I am all too aware of the imperfection of the following pages. In placing this book before the public I am confident that those who may be persuaded to use the methods described hereafter will not regret the experiment, and what is more, will find the measure of their success and pleasure increased a hundredfold. Light fishing is now out of its infancy and will, I wager, soon oust completely the ancient methods to which the fisherman in India holds so tenaciously.

In these hard times when money is scarce many are put off by the expense of buying new tackle. I have therefore set out to make the fisherman who will use the tackle described as self-dependent as possible, and I even claim that he can set himself up for a modest sixty rupees.

I have to thank my friends for much help in reading through proofs and in helping me with their greater experience. In particular my thanks are due to Major W. E. Dean, 12th Frontier Force Regiment, Mr. A. M. David, I.F.S., Capt. G. Eustace, 12th Frontier Force Regiment, and to Mr. G. Perry Duprey, M.R.C.S., L.R.C.P., for Diagrams 1 and 2, and to Mrs. M. Adie for Diagram No. 8 and her photograph "The Gaff Stroke."

The reproach of the shikari and particularly the fisherman is a predilection to the anecdotal; this I have tried to suppress most rigorously. Proven fact is what we all want, and it is this I am now at pains to put forward in the following pages.

Heather Patch Cottage,   C. W. W. S. CONWAY.
Cross-in-Hand,
Sussex.

❊❊❊❊❊❊❊❊❊❊❊❊❊❊❊❊❊❊❊❊❊❊❊❊❊❊❊❊❊❊❊❊

CONTENTS

ILLUSTRATIONS

The

Environment & Angler's Club

43, Golf Links, New Delhi-110003
Ph.: 4690654, 4616473
Fax: 91-11-3720391

Foreword

H ere is an old book that commends the virtues of fishing with light tackle and compares the two basic varieties of spinning reels, the fixed spool and the multiplier. Technology has travelled far but the logic of light tackle and comparison of reels holds true even now. Today we are able to perform the same functions with much lighter tackle as lines are thinner, rod and reels lighter and more efficient. This gives a basic advantage to the modern angler as he can cast further, play harder tirelessly and maintain a more sensitive contact with the fish. However, there is a tendency to go even lighter as it becomes more sporting but a point is reached where such lightness prolongs the fight and makes the fish overexhausted for releasing. Multiplier reels with their smaller free spools and direct drive offer a mechanical advantage for longer casting and playing big fish and now that they have virtually overcome back clash problems they are highly recommended.

Capt. Conway's detailed explanations of basic and terminal tackle can help many anglers understand their outfits better and decide on the next buy. His theories are still valid as two main factors remain unchanged viz. fish behaviour and water dynamics. Casting techniques are well elaborated. Notes on fish species and advice on tackling them are useful.

The credibility of the author is high as he has travelled extensively to the remote corners of India in his study. *Sunlit Waters* is a welcome change from the purely academic books on fish biology as it aims to promote the angler's catch.

(Vijay Soni)
President

Chapter I

THE CASE FOR LIGHT FISHING

FISHING as an absorbing pastime ranks second to none with its devotees. Naturally the pleasure to be derived from it is primarily dependent on successful results. Unlike other sports, however, it does not depend on expertness alone ; to obtain the best results the proper tools are necessary. The circumstances which led me to investigate the possibilities of light tackle in India must have been more or less common to all anglers who, like me, had to seize whatever opportunity that might offer for getting the maximum enjoyment from a casual day's fishing as well as from the pre-arranged expedition, often under conditions far from ideal. For in spite of the most careful arrangements, I fear that, like many others, my leave was often curtailed or put off to another date by some such momentous matter as an inter-company hockey tournament, or a regimental sports meeting, any question of the avoidance of which would have been tactless and indiscreet. All too frequently the halcyon days of spring and autumn would go past without anything but the briefest visit to the water-side, leaving but the hot weather for fishing forays, when exertions with a heavy rod call for a keenness and application not demanded in many other forms of shikar.

And then of the fishing itself. The mighty mahseer – what pictures that phrase conjures up in the mind of the angler in India ! In days gone past nothing but the mightiest tackle was considered fit for the capture of this terrifying monster. Even today quite eighty per cent. of those who fish for him do so with tackle more suited to the shark, or to some other "denizen of the vasty deep", than to a very gallant freshwater fish, whose powers of endurance and fight can best be compared to a salmon of equal weight ; thus do they lose half the fun of the game. Fishing has been termed a gentle recreation, and rightly so ; thus the use of Brobdignagian tackle cannot but be an admittance of ineptitude on the part of the angler. I fully admit that the rivers and hill streams of India are on the whole much faster than those of Europe, but the difference is not so marked that skill on the part of the fisher may be thrown to the winds and pure skull-raking tactics left to take its place. Modern light tackle has more than proved its ability to deal with hard-fighting salmon, trout and sea trout in the fastest of European waters, so why should it not be efficient in India ?

The variety of fishing offered to the fisherman in India is so great that, unless one is the fortunate rajah or rich man of fable, some form of gear must be obtained that will not only give the advantages of light tackle but will at the same time give the confidence of heavier outfit without its weight. My requirements were an equipment which, whilst giving the maximum enjoyment with a gallant pounder, be he trout or masheer, would also be able to deal satisfactorily with a fish of many times that weight. My further requirements were a generally robust construction and the very greatest possible immunity to a tropical climate such as is represented by a Punjab hot weather and the monsoon that follows it, coupled with a general simplicity of manipulation. I also wished for some form of tackle that would enable me to *catch more fish* under the conditions of weather and water peculiar to the north of India.

Fishing possibilities are so limitless in this land of rivers that a lifetime of application would not exhaust them. Further, fishing in India can scarcely be said to have taken its proper place in the field of shikar. Very few have interested themselves in the natural history of fishes ; hence we find that a very real paucity of literature on angling exists. Such as has been published nearly all describe and advocate nothing more than a slavish copy of the old and established methods in use in England. Little or no attempt appears to have been made to try out the more modern forms of tackle which are now making such stride at home, still less to modify them to the needs of the angler in India. The classics written by the redoubtable Thomas and Skene Dhu are regarded as the last word on the sport. Far be it from me to decry in any way the magnificent works written by these pioneers. I cannot but feel, however, that had they had the opportunity of using the light tackle of today they would have been the first to advocate its general use. Their descriptions of fishes, and fishing localities, will remain for many a day to come as standards on the sport ; and their ability in the field of natural history must always give their works a welcome on the bookshelf of the fisherman in Northern India.

I am told that there exists in the Punjab a Research Branch of the Fisheries Department, but I regret to say that at no time have I seen any of its publications. If any original work has been done, or useful information collected dealing with the diet, spawning habits and distribution of the better known species of fish, it should be advertised and made available to the public. At no time has there been a greater number of keen fishermen in the Province than at present, and we are all of us thirsting for information, which only the Fisheries Department can give.

The fish population of the average Indian stream is enormous, and yet how often does one see the angler wade straight into a stream the moment he arrives, sending hundreds of small fry scurrying hither and thither all over the pool, frightening their elders and betters and so reducing the fisherman's chances of sport to an almost irreducible minimum. And why, may we ask, does he do this ? For no other reason than that he is not able to cover the best lies for good fish. They are just too far off for successful casting. The advent of the threadline and the American Level Wind Multiplying reels makes long casting possible, nay, even easy, to the veriest tyro. But a long cast in itself is about as much use as a long prayer if other factors are not considered.

I hope it will be generally acknowledged that clear water spells the best chances of good sport, hence the need of the finest possible trace or cast and reel line must be a *sine qua non* to success. The nearer we can get to complete invisibility of the line and the cast to the fish, the more likely are we to deceive him. Floods and dirty water make fish sick and put them off their feed. The objection to the very clearest water is only based on the fact that the fish are more able to see the angler at a greater distance and are therefore more easily disturbed than at other times. On the other hand, the fish themselves will be able to see the bait at a greater distance and therefore each cast covers a potentially feeding fish.

As we all know, every stream fish has to lie in the water with its head upstream in order to allow water to flow through its gills ; it stands to reason, therefore, that an approach from its rear (i.e. downstream) and casting upstream allows the fisher not only to approach his quarry unseen but to present his bait in such a way that the fish will regard it as a natural phenomena and not just something to be investigated with care. To take a concrete example, a small fish in a hurry is more likely to make a rush downstream when it is frightened than to laboriously fight its way against a strong current. That "whale" which you hope to hook knows this, too, and is therefore more likely to take your bait when it is behaving in a natural manner than otherwise. Yet in nearly all books the intending angler in India is advised to "cast across and down-stream," a course which would only result in the bait being dragged upstream in the most unnatural manner.

Lest the above statements be misunderstood, let me hasten

to add that I am fully aware that small fish, or, for that matter, fish of any sort, do not normally swim downstream if they can avoid it. In fact, they rarely turn round but usually allow the current to "float" them, down. This is obvious, as a fish prefers to have water through its mouth rather than through the back of its gills. But, when in a hurry or frightened it will swim downstream, and it is the frightened fish which we set out to imitate with our bait. Therefore, let us amend the advice of "down and across" to "upstream and across." The multiplication of the reel will cope with the speed of the stream, and the taking fish, who will be poised in the water with head upstream, will in most cases be hooked in the side of the mouth, where it is almost impossible for him to eject or work out the bait.

Why, you will now ask, has not this obvious truth dawned on expert fishermen before now ? They certainly appreciated the fact that upstream casting would, without doubt, result in better catches, but how was this to be achieved when every attempt ended in a bird's-nest of line or the bait becoming snagged as the angler was not able to recover it fast enough ? The nett result was that anglers took to using reels of a very large diameter in order to give them the rapid recovery of line that they so much desired. We see that many of the most successful reels had a diameter of as much as five inches ; now, a five-inch metal reel is hardly a dainty instrument, especially on a light or medium rod, but quick recovery one must have. Hence we find that, though great strides had been made in producing rods much lighter in weight, further progress was retarded, as a really light rod became an impossibility when coupled to these enormous, heavy reels.

Eventually the happy day dawned when the threadline and level wind multiplier were invented. Light reels with small drums carrying what appeared to be almost impossibly fine lines. With them the time-worn fishing adage of 'fine and far off' at long last became realisable. With them also comes a very real reduction in both size and weight of rods, for the old heavy rod is entirely unsuited to the gossamer-like lines employed.

Change, however, is ever regarded as something to be treated with suspicion ; in this case probably on account of the fact that the older school of anglers felt that, having served a long and arduous apprenticeship in learning how to manage their massive poles and winches, they were being done out of the security of a hardly attained goal by the newer entry who could both outcast and outfish them with very little apprenticeship to the sport. We all of us have our vanity, and when we see a beginner in the field of fishing doing a lot better than ourselves it is understandable if we feel a little piqued. Thus it is not difficult to understand that a prejudice arose against the threadline fixed spool reel and the multiplier. Both were at first regarded as purely pot-hunters' engines, whilst many tackle-makers of repute refused to take them seriously. But it was soon seen by some anglers in this country that both the threadline and the level wind multiplier have advantages which, for Indian fishing conditions, far outweigh their defects.

Much has been said of the necessity of having many yards of line to play with on your reel, particularly when mahseer fishing. In one treatise which I have by me as I write, the author lays down that a minimum compatible with safety is some two hundred and fifty yards. Yes, with the old type of rod with perhaps a minimum length of ten feet this was very necessary, as even with the strongest of them the maximum strain which the rod could exert was a mere pound and a half when the critical curve was reached. Reliance was placed on the pliant top of the rod to play the fish, to take when he gave and to give when he took. The reel was a secondary consideration altogether, due to the fact that unless of a very large diameter it was incapable of sufficiently rapid recovery of line to keep pace with the mad rushes of the fish. In the case of the level wind multi-

Plate II   LIGHT TACKLE—THE PROOF OF THE PUDDING

plier the line capacity is still there, as most of them will hold at least one hundred and fifty yards of ten or twelve pounds breaking strain line. The reason is, however, entirely different. The line is wanted only as a reserve against such trials to patience as unavoidable breakages due to snags and other misfortunes, and the fact that these fine lines wear out faster. In the case of a threadline stationary drum reel a mere hundred yards is more than ample. The secret of the success of this light tackle is found in the two words : constant strain. With the powers of rapid give and take that they allow, a constant and more or less unvarying strain is kept on the fish. Terror seizes him and he plays madly, getting not a moment's respite as long as the fight lasts. With the tackle I advocate, the strength of the reel line and trace can be used to its maximum, and, believe me, a very real strain it is, too.

The heavy line advocated in days past, with perhaps a breaking strain of even up to twenty-five or thirty pounds, was not needed to deal with the fish, but to obviate breakages caused by snags and rocks in the river itself, which the fisherman was powerless to avoid when he had out a long length of line and at the end of it a strong fish which he could not manage for fear of breaking the rod top. Modern light tackle, as described in these pages, sets out to play the fish near at hand and succeeds remarkably in so doing. The faster a fish fights the sooner will be become exhausted.

I am no champion of playing a fish for hours on tackle so light that it is only a matter of time and providence before the dreadful exhibition is over. I like to kill my fish reasonably swiftly, and I hate to see the case of a fish playing the man. To me the story of a man playing, say, a twenty-pound fish on the finest of threadline outfits for a period such as four hours is terrible to a degree. (You may laugh, but this actually happened a few months ago). Few will try to deny an angler his fishing, but there are many who will rightly question anyone torturing a fish for hours on end. A fish only "plays" because of his terror of the unknown which has him fast, and I ask you, my masters, what is torture if it is not protracted terror ? Hence, if I persuade you of the efficacy of fishing light as the result of reading this book, and I hope I do, please remember that it is not sporting to carry it to too great extremes. If you intend to fish for trout in the hill streams of Kashmir, Kangra or Kulu, I do most strongly recommend the adoption of the threadline. The same applies to fishing for mahseer where the maximum weight will not exceed twelve pounds or so. If, on the other hand, you intend to do your fishing where the big fish are expected, which is generally where the great rivers emerge from the hills and where you will have plenty of rough broken water rapids full of boulders and deep strong runs over gravel, then use the steel rod and the multiplying reel.

This book is written primarily for those who will do their fishing for the most part either in the hills or in the foothills, and though much of what I say is applicable to all Indian rivers throughout their course, and may be applied to many fish other than those I mention, it is especially for the fisher in the hill streams that I write

> "Where woods and streams make pleasant dreams
> For weary minded men."

All of us here in India are only beginning to take the fishing possibilities of the country seriously. It is a sport which is eminently suited to the "weary worker on the plains" ; harassed you may be by health, wealth, the colonel, or the family, a few days' fishing away from all of them is bound to soothe. It has about it an undying charm and a singular restfulness that never fails to appeal.

Finally, a word to my future critics – and I fear there will be not a few. Many decry the use of light tackle on the grounds that it makes fishing too easy and that the fish doesn't get a square deal. I do most certainly claim that with the fishing tools described in this book you will, without doubt, catch many more fish than with the old-fashioned tackle. Otherwise I should not have set out to waste your time and mine. Personally, I like to catch fish and plenty of them. I know there are many who appear to glory in what I can only term academic fishing. You know the sort of thing. The day in God's sunshine, the murmur of the stream, perhaps the flash of a passing kingfisher and the perky dipping of a water wagtail, and of course just a few perfectly executed casts in order to remind one that the outing is for the purpose of fishing. Believe me, I too love the beauties of nature and the day in the open, but oh, how very much more do I appreciate them when the tale of fish caught grows steadily more! After all, you needn't kill every fish you catch, nor even, if you wish, any of them. In any case, if you compare the number of fish caught to the enormous number to which you have offered your bait, the result is pitifully meagre.

But enough of all this. Let's cut the cackle and get down to the fishing.

WHEN writing of tackle I am amazed by the variety and quantity on the market. For obvious reasons I cannot and do not intend to advocate the use of any particular make. Where I mention an article by name it is because I consider it typical of its kind.

The majority of fishing done by the angler in India will be in quest of the mahseer. Hence I will escribe first the tackle pre-eminently suitable for his capture ; later I will deal with the threadline, which has, unfortunately, definite limitations.

First, the important matter of rods. Doubtless your mind flies to split cane. For Indian conditions I regret to say that it is *not* satisfactory. I have owned a number of split cane rods, and, though all that could be desired in their pristine newness, they have invariably proved a source of trouble and annoyance as time progressed. In a very little while they all weaken, until eventually there is little or no real power left in them. Some of my rods have had steel centres, but after attending their post-mortems and that of others of their ilk, and seen the steel centre shaken out as rust powder, I sadly but firmly insist that they are also useless as a lasting proposition.

What then ? you ask. Perhaps greenheart will do ? Greenheart, though a longer-lasting material than split cane, also suffers from the climate. After one or two hot weathers the wood becomes too brittle to be reliable. If you must have a wooden rod, I can only recommend a Male Ringall Whole Cane. These bamboos are indigenous to the country and as such are to a great extent impervious to its extremes of climate.

They are easily made up into a very pleasant rod by the fisherman himself, or may be bought ready mounted from any good tackleist in India. They are both cheap and reliable and very pleasant to fish with.

With all wooden rods the joints are a nuisance ; they are always giving trouble and coming away from the wood. This they will continue to do until a metal for ferrules is discovered which will expand and contract at the same rate as does the wood of the rod.

The rod material "par excellence" for India is STEEL, which may be either solid or tubular. It is quite unaffected by temperature, climate, or that curse of mankind " White Ants." The only bogies with which the owner has to contend are rust and dents. The first can be obviated by careful attention on the part of the angler after fishing, or the possession of a rod of stainless steel ; the second is a hazard of usage and is no more to be feared than the normal wear and tear on a wooden rod. Steel rods are withal very cheap, and a fisherman can afford to buy two for the cost of one split cane of good make, and so have a reserve in time of need.

The action necessary in one of these steel rods is difficult to describe ; whether of the short single-handed variety or the longer two-handed one the requirements are the same. It must be pliant without being too lissome. Its strength must be such that it will cast baits of half to three-quarters of an ounce without strain. Few people realise that the chief factor in the choice of a rod should not be the weight of fish which it is proposed to tackle, so much as the weight the rod will be called upon to cast. When casting, all manner of torsional strains are imposed, whereas when playing a fish the strain is for the great part in one plane. More breaks occur in casting and in freeing snagged baits than on account of fish, be they never so large.

The Short Rod. The ideal short rod for India should be about five feet in length, and somewhat stiffer than the standard American article.

It should have agate or composition rings well protected against damage. The test curve of such a rod, when held at an angle of about 65 degrees and pulling on a spring balance in the same plane, should give a reading on the balance of just over four pounds. The question of an offset handle or not is purely one of individual preference. Both are illustrated opposite. Personally, I like the offset handle as it tends to reduce the line friction through the first ring. Casting with these rods is really delightful and very easy. The line friction during the cast is so very much less than with a longer rod, that a fraction of the manual effort is required to cast the same distance. The moment the rod is gripped it comes to hand as though it had been specially made for you, and the thumb automatically takes up a position ready to act as a brake on the reel.

Exponents of the older methods of fishing often argue that with so short a rod it is impossible to follow a running fish, if any obstacles such as high bushes have to be negotiated. Nothing is further from the truth. Before starting to condemn the short rod, just remember that it has little appreciable bend, and it is this bend which limits the effective length of the ten-foot weapon. If in difficulties the short rod may be held high above the head in one hand, which will allow of an effective length of some ten and a half feet for a man of average build.

There are so many rods which meet the above requirements on sale nowadays that to mention any by name would be redundant. If buying a cheap rod, solid steel is safer than drawn tube. Tubular steel, unless the rod is of very good quality, may be unevenly drawn and so have unsuspected weak spots.

The Long Rod. Apart from the Ringall cane mentioned earlier, a longer steel rod than that described above has now been put on the market. The best of these is the "E. MARSHALL HARDY," made by Messrs. Accles & Pollock of Birmingham, and distributed by Milwards of Redditch,

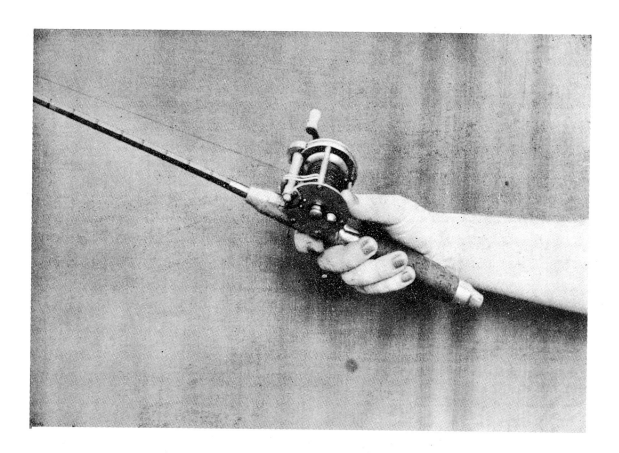

Plate III

RODHANDLES

Above : Straight handle; Below : Offset handle

England. The length of such a rod should be in the region of seven and a half feet and the weight some fourteen or fifteen ounces. Such rods are delightful to use, and meet the case of the man who insists on the two-handed weapon. The great advantage of using one of these rods is that the fisher is able to deal with any mahseer that swims, whereas the short rods are only meant to deal with fish up to fifty pounds.

The Reel. A good reel is the most essential item of the whole outfit. A cheap reel of inferior workmanship is bound to spell disaster sooner or later. To get the best from the short casting rod one must use a Level Wind Multiplier. Here the drum does not carry the handles, and therefore it is possible to make it of a lighter metal than the rest of the reel. Thus, it will cast a lighter bait, drum size for drum size, than will a reel of ordinary pattern, *because the drum can be made lighter than the rest of the reel.* These level wind multipliers are generally of the wide spool small diameter type, which gives less spool momentum and therefore better casting, because there is less tendency to overrun.

The next consideration with regard to these reels is the matter of line recovery. The normal ratio of a turn of the handles to a turn of the drum is four to one. To take a concrete example, the reel I use with a spool diameter of $1\frac{7}{8}$ inches recovers approximately the same amount of line for one complete turn of the handles as would a $5\frac{1}{2}$ inch non-multiplier, the drum being full in both cases.

The reel is normally used on the top of the rod (*vide* illustration), so that one can tell at a glance how much line is out, and in order to be in the best position for the application of a brake on the spool of the reel from the thumb of the angler.

Latterly there has been a tendency to produce level multiplying reels with an adjustable slipping clutch incorporated in their make-up. Personally I deprecate such an innovation. If one wishes to use the ultra- fine lines, why not use the Threadline Coil Casting reel ? The attraction of playing a fish with a level wind multiplier lies in the extreme nicety of brake control which the fisherman exerts on the bobbin of the reel with his thumb. When playing a strong fish in fast waters the successful braking or otherwise of the reel is the success or failure of the battle. In any case, in fast Indian mountain streams the pull on the bait exerted by the water is often so great as to make the maximum clutch setting essential.

The Level Wind Multiplier is often referred to as a purely American invention. In point of fact it was first brought out in England, but met with little or no success owing to faults in design. The Americans took it up and were the pioneers in adapting its use to the short rod. Thus the great majority of these reels on the market are by American makers, though there are a few made by English manufacturers too.

There is usually some form of anti-backlash device fitted in the better models. But until the angler has learnt to use them it is better not to put too much trust therein, such braking of the reel as is required in casting being provided by the angler's thumb. It does not take long to acquire the knack of exerting just that correct amount which is so necessary in order to achieve a good cast, and to prevent overruns.

The line is wound on to the bobbin of the reel evenly by means of the level wind mechanism. Its most usual form is a travelling line guard, moved by a pawl travelling in an endless slot on a spindle of hardened steel. It is a very ingenious device and obviates such annoyances as "line lock" and uneven piling of the line on one side of the bobbin.

These reels need a few drops of oil once, at least, on every fishing day. Not very much to ask, I hope you will agree ; and in return they give years of faithful service. If the reel is by a good maker spare parts are obtainable, and the fisherman in India is strongly advised to carry such spares as an extra pawl and double thread shaft. You never know when a breakage may occur at the water-side, and those hard-won days of a short fishing leave brought to an abrupt end, if replacements are not at hand.

The modern fishing reel of good make is a really beautiful piece of mechanism, and therefore worthy of the owner's greatest care. I cherish mine each as an only child, and after a fishing trip take it to pieces and clean every working part thoroughly. I must confess I take great pleasure in doing so ; my reels are to me old and valued friends and therefore worthy of my utmost care. How often does one see a good reel which the owner has allowed to become filthy and discoloured with neglect, and yet how vociferously will the same owner complain when it lets him down. A clean reel is a joy to use ; and the friendly glint of polished metal that meets the eye on opening the tackle box is both an invitation and a reminder of happy days.

The Line. The Line for use with the short rod and the Level Wind Multiplier should be as fine as is consistent with a breaking strain of from ten to fifteen pounds. It should be hard plaited to avoid stretch and may be braided. The beginner should use a line of fifteen pounds' breaking strain, and as he becomes more used to the outfit the strength of the line may be reduced by a pound or two. Always err on the side of fineness in your line and trace, and the measure of your success and pleasure will be the greater.

The best lines are at present made by the American tackle-makers. This is not surprising, as the Americans have for some years past held the field as exponents of the use of the short rod for taking ALL types of game fish. Examples of these lines are the deservedly famous _Lignum Vitae_, and the _Pfleuger Nonpereil_. Both these, though water-proofed, are not dressed lines in the strict sense of the word.

When fishing is definitely "off" and tackle has to be put away, don't

❧ 15 ❧

leave your line wound round the bobbin of the reel. Wind it off on to a wooden winder and put it away in a drawer with camphor or mothballs. Many a good line has been ruined by being left about so that the insects with which the East abounds are able to half eat through a few strands, which damage is probably overlooked, with disastrous results eventually. Remember it is always the best fish that gets away, and that is no joke invented by some poisonous trite pedantic scoffer at the gentle art, but a terribly true statement of fact ! I have read the advice that a line may be left looped round a nail on the wall. Don't believe such a fantastic story. It only offers every passing moth a free meal, apart from other forms of damage that may accrue from rust and moisture in damp weather.

Of the remaining et ceteras of the fisherman's outfit I have little to say. Some like to use a gaff and some a landing-net. Personally I prefer a gaff ; it is easier to carry about, and, if fixed to a good iron-shod bamboo, makes a very good wading staff. Actually the coolie one picks up at the water side soon learns to be an expert at landing a fish by getting a grip behind ·the gills, after you have persuaded it into a shelving beach, even in the case of the largest fish.

Tackle-makers' catalogues offer tackle boxes in profusion. Some are very useful, some useless, and some are a damned nuisance. The angler must decide for himself what his requirements are. For years I managed very successfully with a series of old Barney's Tobacco tins and the smaller variety of biscuit boxes, which I housed in a capacious fishing-bag. Now I have but one tin box with a hinged lid and a tray in the top. It carries all my requirements, and fits into a more modest size of bag, which allows of the attendant coolie being loaded up with better commissariat arrangements and perhaps such things as a bathing-dress and towel. One of the greatest appeals of fishing in India is that you may cut down to a minimum the horde of sycophants such as beaters, shikaris, and so on which are such an unescapable adjunct to other forms of sport. In fishing the success or failure of the trip is to a great extent dependent on you, when and where to go, the baits to use, and the type of water most likely to hold taking fish. The satisfaction of solving these problems unaided is enormous.

Now that we have described the essential paraphernalia of the angler, and before going on to the details of baits and so on, I feel that we cannot do better than learn how to cast

To catch fish of all kinds accuracy and ease of casting under all conditions are a "sine qua non" to success. To those anglers who would have mastery in awkward places and under all varying conditions, the short rod and level wind multiplying reel is truly a gift from heaven. It is really amazing the number and variety of casts which can be made with such an outfit. First and foremost, the overhead cast, throwing the bait high into the air. This is the most essential to master. Then we have the forehand drive, wherein the arm and shoulder muscles come into play ; and finally the forehand and backhand wrist flicks which, with the minimum of effort, send the bait in a rising plane across the water. Yet again we have the casts which are peculiar to the double-handed rod.

A written description of how to cast must perforce be very incomplete, and I therefore crave your indulgence if my explanations fall short of complete clarity. I do, however, wish to impress on you that the whole matter is not nearly so difficult as it would appear.

Casting is best *not* learnt by the water-side. Good casting is an art, and like all arts it is only learnt as the result of practice. Therefore, before embarking on a public exhibition, let us learn the rudiments in the fastnesses of our own home ; so we will start, shall we say, on the garden lawn or the tennis court, with a half-ounce weight attached to the end of the fishing line. Academic fishing, if you like, but very necessary.

c

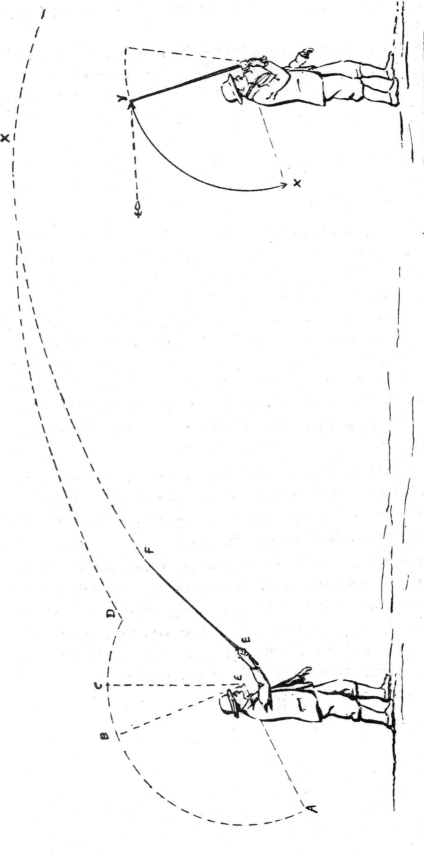

Fig. 1. CASTING WITH THE SHORT ROD Thick line X. Y. represents the Power Stroke

Fig. 2. CASTING WITH THE SHORT ROD
A. The Start of the cast;   B.   End of power stroke
C. D. Simple follow through; E. Position of hand for simple overhead cast.
F. Position of rod tip when arm is extended
E. Hand and arm extended for greater Length of cast.   Cuts out angle at D.
X. Bait begins to drop here, apply a little thumb pressure on reel to prevent overrunning

First, the overhead cast. To achieve it, put the rod over your shoulder with the bait hanging eighteen inches from the rod point and the reel locked by pressure from the thumb. Now bring the rod forward smartly, releasing the thumb pressure just before the rod becomes vertical. The rod point must not be allowed to pass *beyond* ten degrees from the vertical. Try to throw the bait as high as you can ; this will obviate any tendency to slam it down in front of your feet. The bait (in this case the lead weight) will follow a parabolic trajectory through the air. When the maximum height of the curve is obtained and the bait begins to drop, apply a little light pressure with the thumb to prevent overruning. In Figure 1 the power stroke of the cast is shewn by the thick line X–Y ; the rest is a follow-through. Figure 2 shows the whole cast from start to finish. Once the elements are mastered the arm may be extended to its full length in the follow-through movement, which cuts out the angle at D (Fig. 2), so that arm, rod and line form a continuous straight or nearly straight line, with the result that a minimum of line friction occurs. By thus straightening the arm, the length of the cast is considerably increased. The fisherman should, after a little practice, be capable of achieving a distance of about forty yards quite easily. Great strength does not "return the penny" in casting. A smart power stroke followed by a correct follow-through gains the object "every time a winner." As efficiency increases, then – and only then – start trying for accuracy. Place an aiming mark on the ground and try to hit it. Accuracy is easily obtained in overhead casting, as only two diamentions are concerned ; the beginner will surprise himself how soon he will land his lead weight right on the aiming mark.

From the foregoing you will appreciate that casting is possible in the most confined spaces – an advantage which cannot be overstressed when fishing some overgrown jungle streams in the hills. After a little practice the angler will learn to cast from almost impossible positions. In passing,

I may say that I have actually killed a fish whilst lying full length on a rock in mid-stream, as it was far too slippery to stand on.

In the case of the overhead cast, and, for that matter, in all forms of casting, I very strongly recommend that anyone should learn to cast both right and left handed, and to cast with whichever hand is nearest the water's edge. Good and accurate casting will then be possible, no matter what annoyances and obstructions are at hand to try one's patience.

I do not propose to attempt description of the other casts mentioned for use with the short rod in any detail. I feel that the average man, once he has mastered the overhead cast, will find little or no difficulty in executing the forehand drive or the wrist flicks without outside help.

The wrist flicks, whether right or left handed, are intended not for distance but to search all likely holding water within a radius of about twenty-five yards. There is no power stroke and follow-through in the case of the flicks. The action is just a smart and quick flick as though you were trying to get rid of a blob of mud on the end of your rod. The angler will stand more or less facing the aiming mark and vary his casts in distance and direction as the occasion demands.

In the case of the forehand drive, the intention of the angler is to get the bait far out, hence a long power stroke is required. Now, once the element of strength is introduced the tendency is to use too much, and to land the bait well past the aiming mark either to the left or right. Thus for this cast the fisherman will not stand facing the aiming mark, but should point his shoulder towards it and cast with the hand furthest away. The diagram shews the movements for a forehand drive when the right hand is used.

When the rod tip is at A, it should be about level with the angler's knee ; as the power stroke progresses the rod tip should rise, so that when it reaches B it is level with the angler's waist. In the follow-through

Plate IV　　　　　TWO HANDED CASTING
Above : Start of the Cast ; *Centre* : Release Thumb Pressure : *Below* : and Follow Through

movement from B to C the rod tip should not be allowed to rise any more.

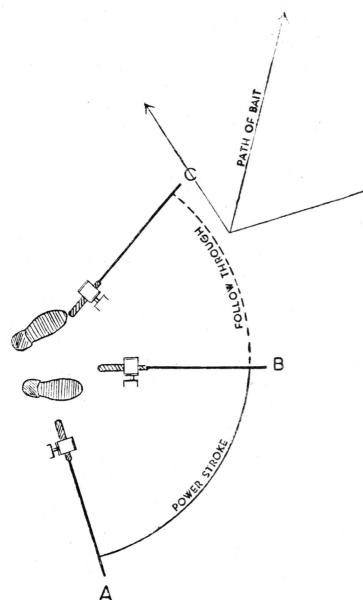

Fig. 3 : THE FOREHAND DRIVE

If you are using a two-handed rod the actions for the overhead cast are exactly the same as for the single-handed rod, the only difference being that the rod is gripped with both hands.

A successful side cast is not so easily achieved, however, and a combination of the overhead and the side casting movements takes its place. Stand slightly inclined from the place where you wish your bait to fall, rod rings up, check off, and your thumb braking the reel. The bait should be hanging about one yard from the rod tip. Now drop the rod point a little and, slightly flexing the knees, swing the bait in the direction you wish it to go with a half overhead, half side movement. As the rod reaches its highest point release the thumb pressure on the reel and let the bait go. Brake the reel again slightly whilst the bait is in flight to prevent overrunning. Half an hour's practice will given you a fair mastery of this cast, and it is not unduly difficult to achieve a fair degree of accuracy in a comparatively short period. At the end of the cast the rod point should be directed at the spot to which the bait has been thrown, and as the bait nears the spot apply thumb pressure, and it will enter the water with the minimum splash. Always avoid banging your bait into the water in all casting. Aim your cast a little above or beyond the exact spot you wish to hit, and as the bait is about to pass over thumb the spool of the reel so that it will drop lightly where you wish.

The Threadline Outfit. What exactly is "threadline"? The analogy is to the domestic sewing-thread, and as the thickest corresponds to the line with a six-pound breaking strain, I submit that such is the strongest line that may be used successfully, before the lightness of the tackle is lost sight of. Such a line limits the use of this gear to conditions where you will not have to deal with fish of much over a dozen pounds in weight and where you will not have to contend with the full force of a great river possibly in flood. Other provisos to successful threadlining are that the bed of the river should be reasonably clear of snags, and when into a heavy fish that it is possible for the angler to follow up or down the bank. Hence the use of the threadline may be limited, as far as mahseer are concerned, to the clear streams of the hills or in places where the fish are not of the largest variety. For trout-fishing in Himalayan streams I venture to suggest that there is no form of tackle which can equal it.

The threadline reel and the multiplier are not normally interchangeable.

THE LIGHT FISHER'S OUTFIT

They are both light fishing gear, but each has its proper province. That a definite overlap occurs under certain conditions I will not deny, but to get the most out of the fishing the Punjab offers, the fisherman is advised to have both types of gear. If you are unable to afford both types, consider carefully the streams you will fish and make a choice accordingly.

The Rod. The rod for use with the threadline should be about seven feet in length and mounted with agate or porcelain rings throughout. Its action should be slightly stiffer than that of really stiff dry fly rod. Unfortunately makers do not seem to have been able to manufacture a really satisfactory steel rod for use with the coil casting reel. A good ringall will answer well, but when mounting it remember to fit it with enough rings, which in the upper part should be not less than eight inches apart. As the baits which are used with the threadline are so light, and the strains to which the rod is put so controlled on account of the slipping clutch in the reel, a split cane rod may be used with greater success than with the heavier tackle. Of course trouble with the rod ferrules is bound to occur, and a falling-off in power on the part of the rod does arise, but it is not so marked as with other forms of tackle.

Alcocks offer two suitable rods, which I have used and found delightful. They are the "Light Caster" and the "Nimrod." The former is for use with the finest tackle, and the latter is quite capable of managing fairly large fish comfortably.

The Reel. Coil casting or threadline reels are suitable to the very lightest forms of fishing. In them the bobbin of the reels is set at right angles to the direction of the cast and recovery of the line ; furthermore, the drum does not revolve in casting. Hence, fears of an overrun are entirely eliminated.

In his writings on the threadline Mr. Alexander Wanless has laid down the following essential qualifications for the reels :—

✿ 23 ✿

a.   A multiplying action which enables rapid recovery of the bait with a small drum.

b.   A method of altering the tension of the reel instantly and at will.

c.   A device which distributes the line evenly over the drum, so effectually preventing locking.

d.   A slipping clutch which enables the use of the very thinnest possible lines.

The most necessary qualification of them all is the slipping clutch.

There are many reels on the market which combine all or some of the above qualities – some cheap, some not so cheap, and some at truly luxury prices.   I feel that I cannot do better than mention the names of three which, between them, cover the whole run.   The first is the "Allcock-Stanley," which is perhaps the most popular coil casting reel today.   I understand that the manufacturers have now made and sold some 10,000, a fact which speaks for itself.   This is a delightful little reel, though limited to use with the finest lines, as it has a small capacity for line.   For anyone who is fortunate enough to do most of his fishing for trout, I venture to state that I believe there is nothing to beat it for simplicity and long service.   The second reel I mention is the justly famous Illingworth.   As marketed nowadays it is the direct descendant of the original threadline reel invented by the late Mr. A. H. Illingworth in 1905.   It is a beautiful piece of mechanism, with very few parts that can go wrong, The last of my trio is the Felton-Crosswind.   It is made by Allcocks of Redditch, and is perhaps the most perfect of all the coil casters.   The inventor has, by means of a very ingenious criss-cross winding of the line on to the spool of the reel, entirely eliminated line kink.

The Line.   The ordinary line for spinning use is no good at all with this outfit.   A special undressed, lightly-waxed silk line is required for bait fishing with and without a float.   For spinning, on the other hand, one should use a gut substitute line, as it cuts down to the minimum the line kink bogey. But the gut substitute must be of the very best quality. Sad experience has taught me that much of the stock offered, particularly in the finest sizes, is unreliable and totally unfit for threadline spinning. This is very marked in India, where many dealers allow gut substitute to lie in their shops for many months and in some cases years on end before selling it to the unsuspecting fisherman. All gut substitutes should be soaked before use – a very important point ; otherwise a single kink, and the fish of the year goes on his way rejoicing. Soaking is very easily accomplished, if the spool is taken from the reel and the whole thing placed in a tumbler of slightly warm water. Whilst speaking of gut substitute I feel I cannot do better than recommend to the angler Hardy's Lion Gut Substitute, and the gut substitute sold by the makers of the Illingworth reel (The Light Casting Reel Co., Ltd.) It is important with coil casting reels that the line should just fill the spool but never beyond the lip, as the nearer to the lip the more readily will it extend itself.

The finer the line you use the greater the casting range of the reel, for a fine line empties the spool to a smaller degree and therefore offers less frictional surface to the traverse of the lip than does a thicker line. This applies equally to the silk line as to the gut substitute.

I find that for normal trout work lines with a breaking strain of about two to three pounds, whether of gut substitute or silk, are very pleasant. If, on the other hand, you are out for mahseer up to some dozen pounds in weight, it is best to use one with a breaking strain of four to six pounds. Anything thicker than this rather detracts from the beauty of the threadline as its chief attraction is its very lightness.

Casting. With threadline tackle there is nothing easier than casting. But please don't run away with the idea that because it is easy there need be little or no application on the part of the fisherman. To be a successful

D

threadliner you want to be able to cast your bait *anywhere*. The best fish lie in those places where it is most difficult to angle for them ; under some overhanging foliage, for instance, or in a small backwater no bigger than the top of an umbrella covered by some special sort of a snag put there by Almighty to worry the poor fisherman. Although on first appearance casting is so very easy that you are tempted to go straight to the water-side, fight down the desire and get so adept at throwing your bait on the lawn or tennis court that you can count on dropping it into a soup-plate or some such aiming mark seven times out of ten under all sorts of conditions. With the very fine lines you are now using, any hope of freeing a snagged bait with the aid of a little gentle force is remote, if not quite non-existent. So if you want to keep your tackle, practise with your casting until you feel you can cast almost anywhere.

To cast, take the line off the flier of the reel and rest it on the fore-finger as in the first of the photographs opposite. The bait should be hanging two or three feet below the rod point. For a side swing cast—and I may say that this covers all the essentials of all casting with the thread-line—point the rod not more than at right angles to the line of the cast and horizontal to the ground. Now bring the rod point forward firmly and with a slightly upward movement, finishing with a flick such as you would use to flick some mud from the end of a walking stick. Again I would remind you that great strength does not return the penny ; the secret of any sort of casting is the correct movement smoothly carried out, and with a proper follow-through. Just as you make the final flick release the finger pressure on the lines and the bait will fly out in the required direction.

Any method of casting may be used to suit particular circumstances and your own feelings in the matter. Cast may be backhanded, fore-handed, just an underhand lob, or overhead. You may even use the play

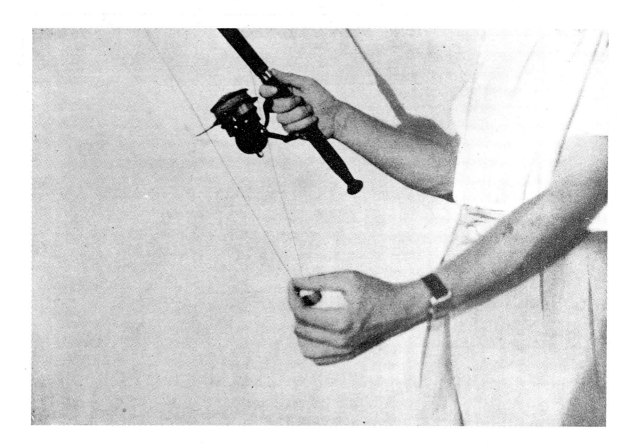

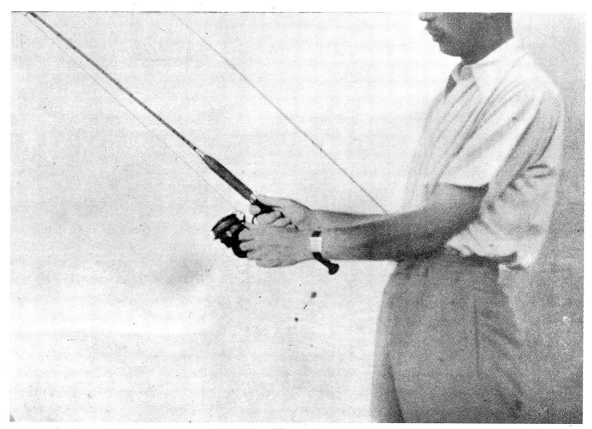

Plate V   THREADLINE CASTING

Above: Take the line off the flier of the reel and rest it on the forefinger.
Below: The line is arrested by turning the handle of the reel.

of the rod to catapult the line in a difficult place, and it is very surprising how far out you can get your bait in this manner.

At the end of the cast, or just before the bait reaches the water, extend the forefinger and pick up the line and replace it on the flier, if your reel is of the finger pick-up variety. If it is fitted with an automatic pick-up the line is arrested by just turning the handle of the reel.

All the foregoing will probably appear a little involved and hard to understand, but once you have the rod and reel in your hands it will prove very simple.

Another form of casting with the threadline reel is to use both hands. Here the line is stripped off the real with the left hand and the cast made with the right hand in the ordinary way. During the flight of the bait the line may be arrested at any time and rehooked on to the flier with the left hand. This is not possible with the automatic pick up reel. On the whole I consider that the finger pick up reel is the better proposition of the two. It has less to go wrong and in the end gives one a greater freedom in casting.

Of other impedimenta for use with one of these outfits there is little to say, except that a landing net is absolutely essential. The tackle is so fine that one cannot risk any sudden jerks and strains which are bound to occur if one relies on a coolie to land the fish. Landing nets are so diverse in character, shape and price these days that I forbear to make any suggestions, other than recommending a beginner to get the cheapest and simplest. It works just as well in the end.

HAT are the reasons for a fish taking a spinning bait? Jealousy, curiosity, high spirits or hunger can all be put forward as motives, and of these I think you will agree that curiosity and hunger alone bear close investigation. The chief characteristic of a spinning bait is flash and colour. It is this flash which causes him to investigate by making an appeal to his predatory nature, and the urge of hunger makes him mouth the bait in order to satisfy himself of its edibility. Compare the case of a small boy at a tea-party, (he certainly is a predatory creature) ; the gaudily coloured cake or ice-cream attracts and is eaten if for no other reason than flash and colour !

To select a bait from a well-stocked tackle box, or from the glowing accounts of a catalogue, is indeed a problem. There are multitudes of spinning baits on the market, but one and all they have been developed from four main types.

First. The Spoon, which rotates by reason of its own curvature.

Second. The metal minnow rotating on account of fins.

Third. The Plug bait, so contrived that it will dart and dive through the water, perfectly imitating the motion of a small fish.

Fourth. The natural fish itself, mounted either as a wobbler or on a spinning flight.

If we accept the necessity of clear water as an essential to successful spinning, it stands to reason that the line must be presented to the fish with as few extraneous attachments as possible. Thus the addition of leads and anti-kink vanes must be eschewed as they only advertise the unnaturalness of the bait. We must rely on the lure itself to maintain both depth and position in the water. Such weight as is required must be contained in the body of the lure itself. Thus will the fish's attention become concentrated on the flash of the lure only, and the frequent and unfortunate case of a fish following the lead on the trace obviated.

The mahseer is primarily a bottom feeder. I have examined the stomachs of a number of fish and have usually found the same contents ; a mixture of weed, slime and small stones, with now and then traces of a small fish, and this last more frequently is settled weather. The movements of the smaller fish population of the average Indian steam occurs earlier than the seasonal migrations of the mahseer, usually when the water is fairly clear ; whereas the mahseer is dependent on flood waters for his migrations. During the runs of such fishes as the chilwa and the stone loach, the mahseer prey upon them, and it is then that the cream of mahseer fishing is to be had.

We may, I think, safely assume that the mahseer, though normally a bottom feeder, is not adverse to a change of diet when his predatory habits are aroused by the passage of a small fish near him. I am confident that he will also take a small fish in a sort of "dog in the manger" frame of mind when he is on the feed and the wee creature passes too near the scene of the repast. In support of this argument I quote the following case. A certain keen fisherman of my acquaintance, feeling that the time had come for him to make a really notable capture, anchored to the bottom of the stream a dead buffalo and left it there for a couple of days. Then he spun a chilwa across the lie of the corpse on the morning of the third day, and was immediately rewarded with the capture of a noble fish of the forty-pound mark. Within a very short time after the capture of the first fish he was also fortunate in taking another only a few pounds lighter in weight. So if you know of any old corpses lying in the stream of your choice, approach the area with reverence and spin across it, and perhaps your reward will be as great !

I am, however, getting away from the point of our argument, which is to discuss the best types of spinning baits. Earlier I stated that all spinning depended on four main types of bait. To take them in the order given, first the spoon.

The spoon is a blatant lure ; its flash advertises its presence most decidedly. It is therefore most successful in the extremes of deep dark water or very shallow water. For fast water the long narrow Norwegian type of spoon, with a comparatively slow rate of spin, is by far the best whereas for deep dark waters the smaller rapid spinning hog-backed spoon holds its own. A hog-backed spoon rides high and in fast waters will often be forced to the surface. Hence it should be made quite heavy for its size and the necessity of a weight on the trace dispensed with. The opposite is the case with the long narrow spoon, and it should therefore be made of thin sheet metal.

Even for the very largest rivers the use of a spoon larger than 3 inches is not worth while. For a beginner I suggest the following quota to start with, which will allow of considerable variety to offer even the most fastidious of fish.

Two Norwegian type Spoons, 3 inches in length and weighing about half an ounce. Colours : one all silver and one all brass.

Two Hog-backed Spoons, 2 inches in length and weighing a shade over the half ounce. Colours : copper and silver and all silver (one of each).

Three Mother-of-Pearl Bar Spoons. Size : one of an inch in length, one of three-quarters of an inch, and one of half an inch. As bought, these spoons are unweighted – but more of this anon.

NOTE. The above weights are those of the spoons mounted with hooks and swivels, etc.

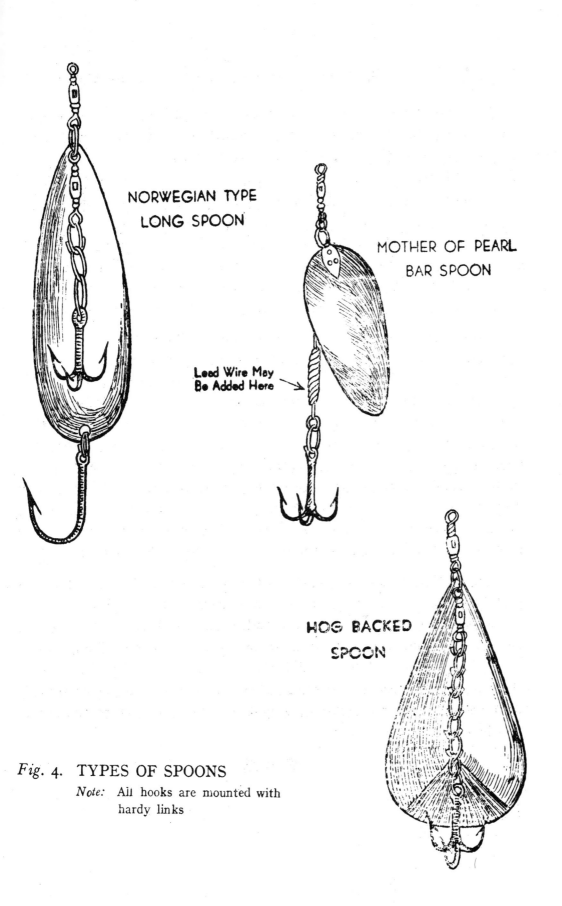

NORWEGIAN TYPE
LONG SPOON

MOTHER OF PEARL
BAR SPOON

Lead Wire May
Be Added Here →

HOG BACKED
SPOON

Fig. 4. TYPES OF SPOONS

Note: All hooks are mounted with
hardy links

The majority of makers mount spoons with split rings. These contrivances, though handy, are very inclined to rust in the centre where it is not easily noticed, with the result that the most infuriating losses occur, both of fish and of tackle.

I feel that I cannot too strongly recommend the use of Hardy's Attachment Links – size 3 is the most suitable for the range of spoons suggested above. Apart from being free from the rust hazard, Hardy's attachment links are very easily attached or detached, and are in every way more manageable than split rings. I carry them joined together in a chain so that if the tackle box is upset I don't lose them in the sand.

Attachment links should be used for joining the hooks to the spoons, and even for making the flying mounts. Figure 4 shews the armament I have found most satisfactory in practice. For the hog-backed spoon a flying mount is all that is necessary ; the addition of a treble to the bottom end of the spoon only tends to interfere with its action in the water. Regarding the big three-inch spoon, which works more slowly, a big single hook (a little short in the shank) attached to the bottom end of the spoon itself is useful in hooking fish which come short, as they so often do in still deep water. Don't forget to put in the swivel at the top of the flying mount in both cases, as it saves the possibility of a fish working a treble hook out of its mouth against the body of the spoon when being played.

The bar spoon has its treble mounted at the end of the bar. This is a useful spoon as the mother-of-pearl part is very light and spins as soon as it touches water. The lead may be adjustable by being in the form of lead wire, and not being part of the spoon proper makes no difference to its action in the water. A bar spoon is the only satisfactory type for use with the threadline, the metal ones being either too heavy for casting, or, if made light enough, have not sufficient weight to get them down to the fish in anything of a strong current.

The most killing colour or combination of colours is a matter which can be decided at the water's edge. Time after time I have tried to work out some conclusions, but have now given up any hope of solving the question. It all depends on the fish. Today we may find that only a brass spoon will kill, yet next week over the same stretch of water and under identical conditions it will never get a touch ; whereas the mother-of-pearl bar spoon is taken avidly. As a general rule use the lighter-coloured spoons in high water and the dull ones for low water. I have never found the least advantage in using spoons with scale markings, though occasionally a red wool tassel on the hooks has a tonic effect on the fish. For hook sizes, a Number 5 Alock's Mahseer treble is a good standard. Hardy's Mahseer trebles I have found to be just a shade too stout, and though they never break or get straightened out, a certain amount of penetrative power is lost on account of their massive proportions. When using a bar spoon with the threadline outfit, do not use the heavy treble hook. With the small strain exerted by the gossamer-light lines and traces the chief requirement is a hook which will take hold with the minimum effort. Hence fine wire treble with needle-sharp points are the order of the day. For a one-inch spoon I use size 7, and for a half-inch spoon a size 9.

Though I have a great affection for the spoon I must admit that it has not normally the killing powers of the plug or dead bait. It has, however, the great advantage of being much more cleanly in use than the natural bait, and is infinitely more pleasant to fish with. A spoon is always ready for use and is mounted on a trace in a moment. They are also very cheap and can be turned out by the dozen by any village brass-worker. Provided a pattern is kept handy they are thus always available throughout the length and breadth of the country ; at a pinch a few copper coins will provide the necessary metal.

And now we come to the second of our types for spinning baits, the artificial minnow. Again we must draw a clear line between those suitable for use with the threadline and those for use with the short rod and the multiplier. Phantom wagtails, etc., are best left alone ; they are merely slavish copies of various well-known baits at home and are not made with any special view to their use in India. They have on occasions all caught fish, but, rather like the vast majority of flies on sale in the large tackleists', are put there in the hope of catching the eye of the angler (and his pocket) by virtue of their colour and beauty rather than to catch fish. Smooth metal devon minnows meet the case very well and are, like the spoon, easily made at small cost by the bazaar metalworker.

For use with the multiplier and short rod I can only recommend the use of a brass reflex devon minnow of about two and a half inches in length. Furthermore, its use is very limited. I use them myself in the very deepest water where light refraction is at its minimum. Under these conditions the flat sides of such a bait make the most use of the little light that exists, and its own weight is sufficient to take it well down to the fish, which are resting probably on the bottom. The weight of one of these reflex flat-sided devons should be from half to three-quarters of an ounce and they should be made of brass. Sometimes it is worth while to have one side silver-plated in order to get the most out of the play of the light down at the bottom of a deep pool.

Devon minnows for use with the threadline should be from three-quarters to one and a half inches in length. Hardy's make a very good range of smooth metal devons, which are available in both right and left hand spins (a real boon to the threadliner as it helps him to overcome the bogey of line twist which is always dogging him, for minnows can be carried in pairs and used alternatively). For the trout streams of the Punjab and for Kashmir I strongly recommended the use of Hardy "Heavyweight" Devons with the threadline. They are specially designed and moulded in a heavy alloy in order to make casting from a stationary drum reel possible, without the addition of any lead on the

❀ 34 ❀

trace. The fins are shaped to give the baits a very rapid spin, and they are marketed in the following colours : Gold, Silver, Blue and Silver, Brown and Gold. A good standard size is the one-inch length which weighs three drachms.

For colours I have found that there is little to touch an all-gold minnow. For me they have killed when all other baits have failed when fishing for trout in Kulu last year. Yet one of my friends using the same minnow failed miserably over precisely the same stretch of water and, not until he changed to a blue-and-silver devon did he start to take fish.

Personally, I am convinced that as regards the colour of baits, CONFI-DENCE on the part of the angler is what really counts. I have always done well whether at home or out here with the inch-long golden devon. Hence I fish better with it perhaps than with any other bait. How strange is the psychology of fishing !

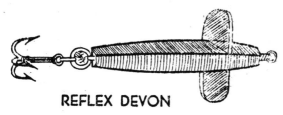

REFLEX DEVON

THREAD LINE DEVON

Note: Both are mounted with a lead so that they will spin freely—Treble hook for the big Reflex Type, but back to back single hook for the Threadline Minnow

Fig. 5. DEVONS

Baby threadline devon minnows should not be mounted with treble hooks. Far fewer hang-ups will occur and far fewer minnows will be lost if the back-to-back single-hook method of mounting is adopted. The illustration here shews what I mean. Hooking with such a mounting is also far more certain and the hookhold itself is also more secure. Spinning with the threadline is at its best when the rivers are at their lowest level and in the very clearest of water. The wee devons should be cast up and across the stream and fished down only a few inches below the surface. It is a system all of its own, and together with that of fishing the plug bait can best be referred to as the "sub surface technique." More often than not good fish are taken in water which seems hardly deep enough to cover them, particularly if the fisherman is out in the early morning and at dusk, when the old cannibals are searching about near the shallow for fry, tadpoles, and frogs.

The third on my list of artificial baits is my friend the plug. For mahseer as a fail-me-never there is nothing which can compare with the plug. It seldom if ever gets hung up, it is easy to cast, its action in the water is a delight to watch, and its fish-getting capabilities are unquestionable. Yes, how very excellent a thing is the plug.

Plugs don't spin. On reeling in after a cast they dive below the surface and *swim* back in a most attractive and natural manner, which exactly imitates a small fish rushing through the water. They have a fatal fascination for Punjab mahseer when the water is clear, and the fish are neither timid nor hesitant in the way they take a plug. Travelling just below the surface as they do the plug exploits the spectacular wild rush of a taking mahseer as no other bait can.

Plugs are normally made of some floating substance or of wood, so that they always float until the action of reeling in forces them below the surface of the water. The speed of their recovery controls within limits the depth at which they swim. Note that plugs dive – they don't sink. They also swim on an even keel and do not spin. No plug used for mahseer fishing should work more than a few feet below the surface.

The floating powers of the plug are often extremely useful ; for instance, a cast may be made into the stream and the bait allowed to float down taking line off the reel, and the lie of a fish reached which would be impossible in the normal course of events owing to overhanging rocks or

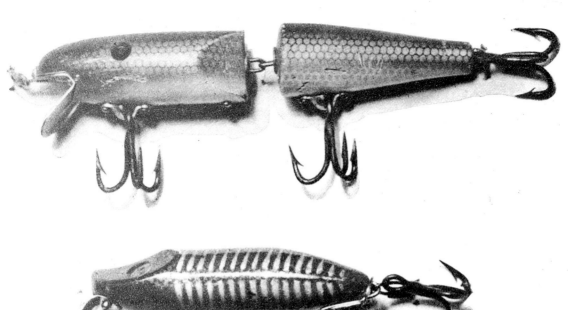

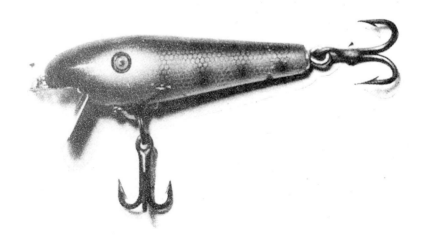

Top : Pflueger "Pal-o'-Mine"
    Jointed 4¼".
2nd : Heddon "River Runt
    Spook Shore Minnow" 3½".
3rd : Pflueger "Pal-o'-Mine"
    Unjointed" 3¼".
Bottom : Hardy Jock Scott
    Wiggler" 2".
All except the last are shewn mounted with
Mahseer Trebles. The "Wiggler" is mounted
with fine wire trebles for thread line use.

Plate VI   PLUGS

trees. Or again, the bait may be cast up and across stream and fished a long distance from where its small entry splash occurred. Many ways of presenting a bait are thus made possible, which adds very much to the interest of fishing and also to one's chances of catching fish. Plugs work down when they are retrieved by the push of the water against the head of the bait – otherwise they float – so that fear of the loss of the bait after an overrun or other such trial of patience is at the very minimum. No lead or swivels are required on the trace, which helps to concentrate the attention of the fish on the bait only. Sinking plugs are obtainable by those who want them, but are of no very great advantage as, under normal conditions, if a mahseer will not take a bait when in mid-water or just below the surface he is not very likely to be interested for some little while.

When the air is warmer than the water, a very normal state of affairs in India, the plug is fished just below the surface, and a rising fish can be seen actually coming to meet the bait ! As the fish turns to go below again draw the rod back with a steady firm pull which will in nearly every case hook the fish securely in the side of the mouth.

Plugs, when bought, particularly if by American makers, are often armed with large size springy tinned trebles which are patently useless for mahseer, and have not even the advantage of really good hooking properties. Such hooks should never be used ; in their place mount the bait with Alcock's Mahseer Trebles (Numbers 4, 5, or 6). Make quite sure that the hooks move freely in order to avoid giving the fish any leverage on the bait when side strain is applied. Here the jointed bait acquires a special attribute.

There is little to choose between the jointed and the unjointed types. Perhaps the jointed models are better in deep water and in fast flowing streams than the unjointed, but such difference as may exist is so little as to be worth further consideration.

In the photograph opposite are a selection of well-known makes which will suffice for the beginner to start with. For those who are neat with their hands and have time to spare (and this is good for nearly all fishermen) a full description of how to make one's own baits is given in Chapter VII. Home-made plug baits can be very killing and have accounted for some of my best fish. In spite of the great number of baits on offer, we have by no means arrived at a stage of perfection in plug design, and there is a great field open to the fisherman who is prepared to experiment and adapt his baits to local conditions.

Plugs for use with the threadline offer something of a problem. So far as I know a really satisfactory *small* pattern has yet to be put on the market. Hardy's have quite a successful range which can be used with the coil casting reel in their "Hardy-Jock Scott Wiggler," but even they are not the last word for threadline use. "Heddon River Runties" are also fairly successful, as they do not offer so much resistance to the water as their bigger brothers, but are a little heavy. I also give a design of my own later in this book, but here again the result is not perfect by a long way. The trouble with the smaller variety of plug is that once a certain size limit has been passed the bait will not remain on an even keel and also loses the provocative wiggle

Finally, as a last word in praise of the plug. I draw your attention to the fact that as it does not revolve when being fished line-kink is at the minimum and consequently the life of the line is greatly prolonged.

And so at last we come to the natural fish itself. Anyone looking through a dealer's catalogue wherein mountings for spinning the natural bait are illustrated will soon come to the conclusion that they consist only of two types. The spinning flight, wherein the bait is made to revolve by means of fins, and the wobbler, wherein the bait revolves in the water on account of a curvature imparted to it. In short, we have the principle of the metal devon and the spoon.

Both spinning flights and wobblers are good. The spinning flight has the advantage of imparting a twist to the line only in a known direction. Thus, if right and left hand spin mountings are used alternatively there should be no fear of abnormal line kink or twist. Wobblers, on the other hand, are difficult to control in the direction of their spin and are therefore somewhat risky. The wobbler is the most natural mounting for dead bait, as a fish moves its body from side to side in swimming, but I doubt if the fish you intend to catch will worry about such refinements.

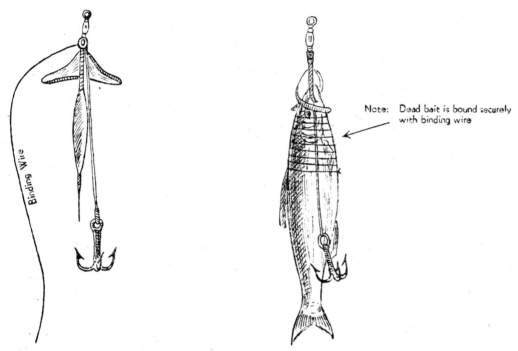

Note: Dead bait is bound securely with binding wire

Fig. 6. MOUNTING FOR NATURAL BAIT.

The illustration above shews the spinning mount I use, both baited and unbaited. It is easily made up and particulars of how to set about it are given in Chapter VII. I have found in practice that it is better to use a single treble than a huge array of hooks, and it should be placed so

❀ 39 ❀

that it lies below the anal fin and just above the tail of the bait. A Number 5 treble is a most useful size of hook for all normal bait for mahseer. The natural baits themselves should be from two to four inches in length, depending on the weight of fish you propose to catch, when using the short rod and the multiplying reel. For threadline the baits may vary from one and a half to two and a half inches, and only very small wire treble hooks used in the mount.

It is very important that with all forms of mountings for dead bait such lead as is required be contained in the body of the bait. Many expert fishermen state that when the body of the bait is leaded the spin is not so natural and that leads are best placed on the trace some distance from the minnow. I agree to this but consider that the absence of any extras on the trace concentrates the attention of the fish on the bait itself, and so more than compensates for any minor shortcoming in the action of the spinner in the water, apart from making it easier to cast.

There is another form of dead bait mounting which, though a wobbler, is very useful. It has the advantage of being easily made even at the water-side, and, employing as it does but a single hook, has great holding powers. It is a modification of a pattern given in "Where To Fish" by H. D. Turing. Whip a single hook to a few inches of gut substitute (an Alcock's Model Perfect Number 1/0 will do). Now make a loop of about one and a half inches in diameter at the other end of the gut. Be careful to bind the knots, or give them a dab of that excellent commodity Rawlplug Durofix, to prevent them slipping when wet. The other item required is a suitable sized barrel lead to which a wire eye has been fitted.

To mount the bait, first put the hook through its side, imparting a slight twist to the body in odrer to make it spin ; then pass the looped end of the gut through the gills of the bait and out of its mouth, and back

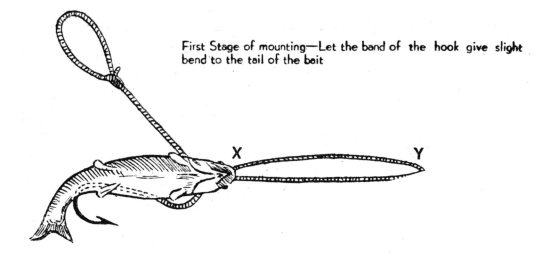

First Stage of mounting—Let the band of the hook give slight
bend to the tail of the bait

Barrel lead with wire eye—The loop of Gut X—Y is passed
through the eye and the lead pushed down the mouth of the bait

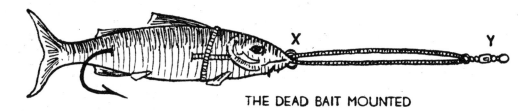

THE DEAD BAIT MOUNTED

Fig. 7. A SIMPLE MOUNT FOR THE NATURAL MINNOW

F

throug h the mouth and out of the gills on the other side.   Next slip the loop of gut over the tail and up the body, and pull on the gut standing out of the bait's mouth.   You will now find that the head of the bait is securely noosed and that a loop of gut stands out of its mouth.   Pass this loop of gut through the wire eye in the barrel lead and push the lead down the mouth and gullet of the bait.   Finally attach the whole thing to a swivel and then to your trace.   A glance at the diagram will make it all clear.

Owing to the lead being so far forward the little fish will now swim and dive in the most lively manner when pulled through the water.

All natural baits are improved by being bound to their mounting with a short length of fine mounting wire.   In the case of the spinning mount I have found it a good thing to attach one end of a six-inch length of wire to the bottom eye of the mounting swivel and bind the bait on with the loose end thus obtained.   The bait is then held securely and does not come to pieces in the water.

For threadline use there is yet another form of mount for dead bait. The Celluloid Scarab, which is a transparent jacket into which the bait fits, and into which it is bound with fine binding wire.   The tackle itself consists, of two fine wire trebles on a loop of gut, and a pear-shaped lead which is pushed into the mouth of the minnow.   The gut loop of the hook mounting is passed through an eye in the lead, the bait being slipped into the jacket so that the hooks lie along its belly.   The whole thing is then made secure with binding wire.

The advantage of the Scarab lies in the fact that when a fish is hooked the bait itself in its celluloid jacket runs up the trace, leaving only the hooks in the mouth of the fish.   Minnows will last a very long time on this type of mounting, and on one occasion I was able to kill no less than four fish without changing or in any way attending to my bait.   The Scarab is essentially a light mounting and should therefore be used only for thread-

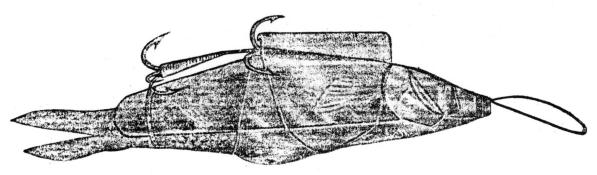

The "Scarab" Tackle Mounted

The Hooks

The Lead

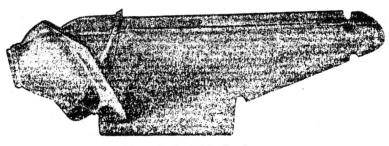

The Celluloid Jacket

Fig. 8. THE SCARAB TACKLE

line work. Once heavy mahseer treble are used it loses much of its attraction and is no more killing than the straightforward spinning mount. Another advantage of using the Scarab lies in the fact that the bright transparent celluloid advertises the bait better and gives it an extremely attractive appearance.

And finally, all that we require now is a trace to form the junction between the reel line and the bait. It is not at all necessary to spend a small fortune on traces. A reel of the finest Killin wire, some swivels, a pair of pliers, and a hank of gut substitute is all that is required. When spinning with the level wind multiplier I always use a Killin wire trace. They are very strong and yet at the same time fine enough to be almost invisible even in the clearest water. The line is so fine that a long trace is not at all necessary. A good standard length is from 18 inches to 2 feet in length, with a small single or double swivel at the junction with the reel line. Swivels are best bronzed, as bright brass ones are very obvious in clear water and glint in the sun in the most provocative manner. I have had a fish go for the swivel before now and evince no interest whatever in the bait which follows it. Don't let the swivels be too large. Hardy's "Hardy Swivel," Size 5, is just about as near perfection in swivel design as I know, and one quite strong enough for use with fine single steel wire traces.

Wire traces are not generally suitable for use with the threadline, though if you propose to do your fishing in windy waters they have their uses as the wire cuts through weeds like a knife. For normal use a gut substitute trace is preferable. It should be about one yard in length and mounted with a double swivel at the top end and a single swivel about a foot down the trace. The tail end of the trace should be finished with a large loop, big enough to slip over any bait that you will use.

Knots and whippings are dealt with fully in Chapter VII, so I will not waste time with them here.

Plate *VII*   MAHSEER—A FISHERMAN'S STORY

Chapter IV

SPINNING PRACTICE (The Short Rod)

*W*E are now all complete in our tackle for spinning, so let's away to the stream of our choice and pit our wits against India's Game Fish No. 1, Barbus Tot, the Mahseer.

To fish for him with any real degree of success, we must have some knowledge of his habits and way of life. Hitting off the right season is perhaps one of the greatest difficulties which face a beginner. Roughly, there are two seasons in the North of India when one may expect the best of the sport. The first is in spring, when the weather is warm enough to get the fish moving and yet not hot enough to melt the snows in the higher hills and bring down the worst of all bugbears to the fisherman : snow water. The second period is when the rains are over and the water has cleared but has not got too cold. This usually occurs in October, though it will depend to a great extent on the monsoon and other local conditions. Fish may be taken with success at other times of the year, but spring and autumn are when the cream of the sport is to be had. I consider that the autumn fishing is by far and away the best. Conditions are then more settled so that one is not in a state of constant fear that, having arrived at the water-side, all hopes of a good day's sport will be dashed to the ground with a view of a turgid muddy stream sweeping along with what appears to be half the soil in Asia held in suspension in its waters. Conditions on an ideal day should appear rather as follows :—

    a.   Clear blue sky.

    b.   Day temperature of about 80 to 90 degrees Fahrenheit.

c. Clear water.

d. Nothing more than a gentle breeze to ruffle the surface of the water.

Snow water is absolutely fatal for the big fish, though the fisher may still get some sport if he uses a bright devon minnow or the small mother-of-pearl spoon on the edges of heavy runs. But on the whole when there is snow water about, any thoughts of serious fishing may be washed out.

In streams which are unaffected by snow water good fishing may be had throughout the hot weather until the rains make the water too dirty. Spinning is best undertaken in the morning for about an hour after sunrise and again in the evening just before and after sunset. During the heat of the day some fish may be taken with bait, provided a careful study is made of the forms of food popular with the mahseer at that particular period. Unfortunately, many of these streams are at so low an altitude that it is often too hot for pleasurable fishing.

Though local conditions make a great deal of difference, I feel that I can safely say that the best period for mahseer fishing in the Punjab are probably from the third week of February to the end of March, and then again for the whole of the months of October, November, and sometimes the early part of December. Mahseer are intensely moody fish and are very sensitive to any impending changes of weather, so the more settled the general atmospheric conditions, the greater are the chances of success.

The mahseer is a migrant ; the object of their periodical movements appears to be that of spawning. Indian rivers and streams, though roaring torrents in the height of the monsoons, become very low (in some cases nothing more than mere trickles) in the middle of the hot weather, and again in the cold weather if there has not been much rain. At the beginning of the monsoon, and for that matter during the whole of it, the mahseer run up the small rivers and streams to spawn, as when in flood these smaller waters offers security from attack owing to the discolouration and a good path of deep water up to suitable spawning grounds. After the rains are over there is a general return down to the bigger rivers apart from a few fish which remain all the year round in the larger and deeper pools of the small streams. As the weather gets colder, and particularly during the coldest months of December and January, the fish all tend to collect in the deepest and largest pools in order to keep warm. On the weather getting warmer again the fish move out into the rapids and run, and here they remain until the snow water comes down, when they change their quarters to the lower-reaches of the smaller rivers, which are unaffected by the melting snow, and to their junctions with the large rivers, until the rains come, and up they go to spawn again. Thus throughout the year there is a constant cycle of movement; so if you know of a place which usually gives very good sport in, shall we say, October, don't be surprised if you can't move a fish there in April.

As regards the lies of the fish themselves, there is one golden rule which all mahseer fishermen will do well to remember. These fish avoid places where the bottom of the river is covered with mud and sand and stick to where the water runs over rocks, boulders and stones. Of course there are exceptions to this rule. One which leaps to the mind immediately is the case of a junction : there is always a certain amount of mud and sand in evidence here, and it is in such places that many of the best fish are taken.

Sometimes it is very easy to ascertain the whereabouts of the fish; for instance, when a run of small fish is taking place the mahseer will all tend to collect where these small fish are in abundance; this is usually on the edges of the streams and in the shallows. Again, on some days when the water is clear the actual lies of the fish may be seen; when this is possible it is well worth while to make a study of these lies and of the behaviour of the fish which are inhabiting them. Notice how a sunken rock affects the surface of the water and how it often causes a swirl or an eddy quite a distance from it. If you can cultivate an under-water mind and an appreciation of the likes and dislikes of the fish, your success as a mahseer fisher is absolutely assured. The "chuck it and chance it" attitude which so many adopt when at the water-side does not give the best results ; the most successful fishers have not the best tackle, neither do they get to the water on the optimum days ; the secret of their success lies in their knowledge of the fish and of how, why, and where it lives. To cultivate such knowledge should be the aim of every fisherman in India, and, for that matter, anywhere else.

Enough of these platitudes, however. Let's get down to our muttons and catch something. We shall assume that the day is in April, the time ten a.m., and we are at a junction of a hill stream with one of the five Punjab rivers. The weather is warm with the promise of the hot weather in the not very distant future ; the Punjab country side, though normally pretty flat and uninteresting, is now at its best, clothed in a mantle of vivid green that belies the arid blasting heat that will come in but a few short weeks. The water itself is fairly clear, as the snows in the higher hills have not had time to melt. If we look at the bank, we shall see that a number of birds are intent on catching some of the endless stream of fry that makes its way up from the main river to the tributary. Here we see four or five egrets wading along in the shallows and every now and again snatching a small fish which gleams like a bar of silver in the sun. Fairy gulls hover and dive, and the best of all fishermen, the Indian pied king-fisher, is intent on taking his miraculous draught. Every now and again the surface of the water is broken by some dozen or so fry which leap into the air as though at the order of some unseen scaly sergeant-major. Keeping well up the bank, and ensuring that our shadows are not cast on the water, we put our tackle together and mount as our bait a River Runt

Spook Silver Shore minnow. We watch for the next commotion on the part of the fry, and after it has been over for about a minute we cast our plug two or three yards upstream of where it occurred. The fry had been jumping in a vain attempt to get out of the way of some large fish who was making a rush at them. The method of the mahseer when making an attack on these shoals of small fish is not to just rush in and grab one. No, he is a greedy fellow, and when he makes his rush he disables four or five unfortunates which he devours at his leisure. We want him to believe that our plug is one of these unfortunates making an unsuccessful attempt to get away down stream, so we retrieve it comparatively slowly. Suddenly there is a wild tug and a swirl in the water and we get a glimpse of an olive-green back, and we are in to our first fish of the day.

Down he comes towards you until he catches sight of you on the bank, when he jinks sideways. Remembering that with this light tackle the secret of success is a constant strain, you have recovered your line as the fish came towards you, and now as he turns you put a strain on him by braking the real with your thumb. No, the strain is too great and you can't hold him; he strips the line off and takes out about twenty yards of it and goes fighting on down stream. Now, your main object is to remain *below* your fish, so that he has to fight against both the strength of the current and the strain that you apply on him with the line. To exert the maximum pull, side strain is applied; this will upset his balance in the water and will tend to force him close to your bank. Soon the rushes get shorter, and the fight resolves itself into a dogged downward boring on the part of the fish; apply all the strain you dare and constantly throw him off his balance. His efforts get weaker and weaker and at last you bring him into the bank and hold him still, telling the coolie you have with you to lift him out. The man rushes at the fish and away he goes again. There is now an interval of swearing on your part, the wretched coolie looks foolish, nervous dogs bark, and your lady friend looks the other way or perhaps even joins in. Well, no damage was done, and you have him approaching the bank again. This time you persuade him on to a shelving beach and the coolie, having in mind your hard words of a few minutes before, approaches warily, and running his hands up the body of the fish gets a grip behind the gill plates and lefts him out. A grand fish of ten pounds in weight. The fight with him has seemed an eternity of alternate hope, despair, and annoyance, but in reality has only lasted some ten minutes. Well, there he is safe and sound on the bank, gasping. Kill him immediately with a hard blow on the head with a stone, and take the hooks out afterwards. No one will deny your right to catch fish, but you have no business at all to make the last few minutes of his life torture while you fiddle about trying to get out the bait from his mouth. Besides, you stand a very good chance of getting a hook into your finger if you don't.

Now let us take the case of a normal pool in one of the larger hill streams, which we shall be fishing, shall we say, in October when all the conditions for a perfect day's fishing are obtaining. I shall name this pool 'Perfect Pool'-it is one which I have often fished and from which I have had some very good catches. Figure 9 shews a plan of it. The arrows represent the current and the way they point the direction of its flow. Rocks are shewn by dark shading, sand by single shading, and stones by little circles.

Fish may be expected throughout the length of this pool in the shelter provided by rocks and large boulders. Don't forget sunken rocks, the presence of which may only be noticed by a hump, or swirl in the water. We may also expect to find fish in the eddies and the backwaters at the edges of the rapids, and again at the tail of the stream where the white water ceases and becomes smooth, especially if there is a corner or rock and some deepish water where a big fish can lie in wait, and watch what the stream brings down. Thus, if we are walking up-stream we might drop in our first cast from point A, dropping the plug just above the corner of

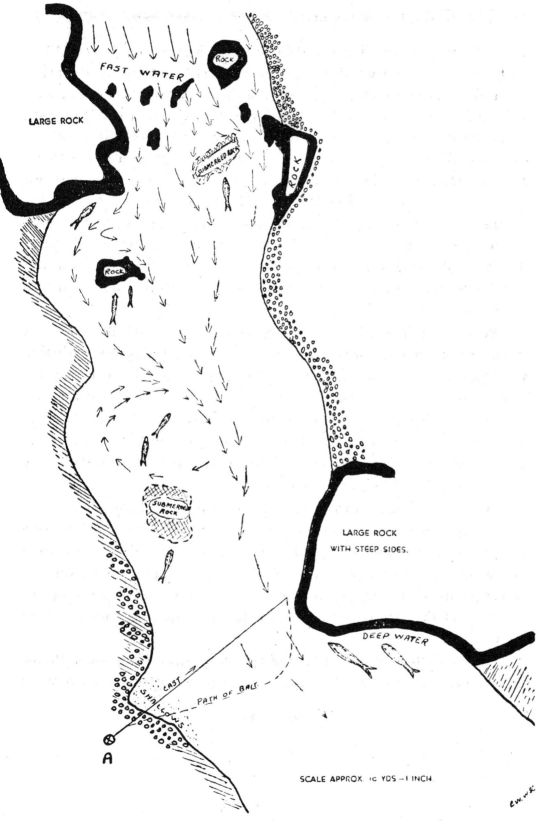

FAST WATER

LARGE ROCK

ROCK

ROCK

SUBMERGED ROCK

ROCK

SUBMERGED ROCK

LARGE ROCK
WITH STEEP SIDES.

DEEP WATER

CAST

SHALLOWS

PATH OF BAIT.

A

SCALE APPROX. 10 YDS — 1 INCH.

Fig. 9. PERFECT POOL

rock so that when we reel it in, it will follow the path, shewn by the dotted line, as the current takes hold of it. The plug should now come downstream, giving the appearance of a small fish in a hurry, and as the current takes hold we put an increase on the pace of its recovery so that it takes a turn across the stream and makes for the shallows. This, I submit, is exactly what a small fish would do, for on rounding the corner his instincts would warn him that he was in danger from the two grandfathers who are shewn as lying near the words "Deep Water," so he would make a dash across the stream in order to get into the shallows where the large fish can't follow. If you execute the cast as described the odds are that by the second or third time of asking you should have an offer. If you hook your fish take him downstream into the pool and play him there, and you will not disturb the water above you.

Perhaps we drew a blank there, so we see straight ahead on our own side a swirl in the water which tells us that there is a sunken boulder which will probably offer a home for a fish. Here our tactics will differ ; we shall cast so that our bait touches the water too or three yards above the swirl. The result is that the fish in the lie suddenly sees a toothsome morsel go flying over his head, and, realising that he must be quick if he is going to get it, rises and takes the plug in a spatter of broken water, and then away down stream into the pool for the fight for life.

Above the sunken rock there is a little whirlpool, and beyond it a rock stands out of the water ; here we cast just above the whirlpool and spin straight down and, after giving it a good try-out, move a little up the bank so that we may cast for the possible fish that lie behind the rock and in the corner just beyond. Finally we cast to a hump in the water just below the fast part of the stream for any stray fish that may be playing about there.

As it is October and the conditions are so good, we shall not waste too much time in any one place but move on after a few casts to each likely lie ;

we can then cover a great deal of water, and where necessary wade the stream to get a better approach to any place which may attract us on the opposite bank. It is really delightful fishing at this time of the year ; and if we go on thus we are also obtaining a wonderful knowledge of the lies of the fish, as we can see everything in the clear water, which will stand us in very good stead later when the water is not so clear. As judgment of where to find fish develops, one attains that happy feeling on some days that each cast made covers a fish !

The home of the good fish is chosen to fit in with the requirements of nothing to do and as much as possible to eat. When bringing your lure near him remember that he is on the watch for some unsuspecting tiddler, so work your lure accordingly. When it approaches a likely lie, exert every effort to make it lifelike ; let it appear like a small fish fighting its way across the current or rushing headlong downstream. Always try and bring your lure from deep to shallow water. This is the natural action of a tiddler, as he is only safe where his larger brethren cannot follow him so he will not normally stay in deep water for fear of a very sudden demise. Always cast into the neck of a pool ; if the inlet of water is broken by rocks so much the better ; regard each rock as the back of an armchair, against which an idle fish may be lounging, so throw your bait up past the rock and spin down, and I hope you will be successful in jogging his elbow.

I am often asked what speed is best for recovery of a spinning bait or plug. There is no best speed ; all speeds are good provided the bait works in a life-like manner. There is one point on which I am perfectly certain : that it is impossible to recover a bait too fast. By this I do not mean that a plug or spinning bait should always be fished fast—far from it ; on many occasions a slow moving bait is more killing by far—but at whatever speed your bait works, it is absolutely essential that it should appear lifelike, and that it should act in the way a live fish would.

Apart from the necessity of the bait being lifelike, it must also resemble the natural food of the mahseer at that particular time of year. For what, then, is the mahseer looking on this October day? They have lately spawned and the winter is approaching, so they are in need of meat. The rivers have now dropped to low level and the ample flood feeding which had been available during the rains is now at vanishing point. With the approach of winter the streams at the higher altitudes will soon become too cold to hold the mahseer, be he little or big, for he hates extremes of climate like the plague. So, feeling the pinch of hunger, and with a rooted objection to sharing his meals with any smaller being than himself, his predatory instincts are aroused and he preys on his own young, the young Kalabanse, and the Stone Loach. All these are silvery fish with a certain amount of darker markings on their bodies. For an imitation of them I find that my old friend the Pfleuger Pal-o'-Mine Minnow takes a lot of beating. The patterns I recommend are the Natural Perch Marking and the Red Side Scale, in that order. Both the jointed and the unjointed patterns are good. If you are out for big fish use the 4 inch jointed model. It has the most wonderfully natural action in the water, and is not too big to take fish of even two or three pounds in weight.

And now the scene changes; instead of fishing in the morning we are out at about four in the afternoon. The evening take is seldom quite as good as the morning for the *numbers* that you will kill; on the other hand, it usually beats the morning on account of the *quality* of your bag. Today we are fishing Blackrock Rapid, of which there is a plan opposite. The water here is on the whole very fast, with here and there a deep dark pool. The coolie tells us that he has seen a fish here a few days before of such proportions that it would appear to be only comparable to an elephant or a battleship. We shall name him Old Faithful, and pray to the gods that tend to anglers' wishes that he will be at home today.

Before starting to cast we spend a minute or two examining the water for signs of life or an indication that Old Faithful is at home. No, I fear there is nothing to give us a line on our plan of action. We know, however,

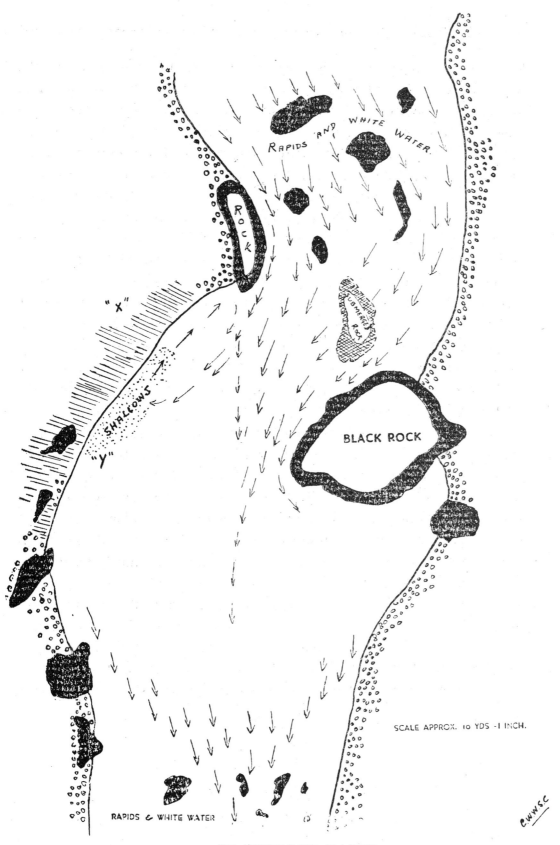

RAPIDS AND WHITE WATER.

ROCK

SUBMERGED ROCK

BLACK ROCK

"X"

SHALLOWS

"Y"

SCALE APPROX. 10 YDS -1 INCH.

RAPIDS & WHITE WATER

C.W.W.S.C.

Fig. 10. BLACKROCK RAPID

from previous observations that big fish are wont to lie in the tail of the pool just where the water becomes shallow before going on down the rapid, at this time in the evening ; hence we try this area first. We will search this place carefully, as very often fish like Old Faithful won't look at the bait until it has been offered them quite a few times, and then take it in desperation, rather in the same manner as you or I would kill a fly that annoys us when we are reading the morning paper. As there has been no response, we next try the shallows along our own bank, casting the bait so that it swims along the line of the deepening water. Still no response. You will notice that we have taken care that our first casts searched all the likely lies on our own bank, and that we have not made ourselves obvious or disturbed the water by wading. Another point which we might remember is that, fishing in the evening, we must take care that we do not get the sun at our back and so throw a long shadow on the water. There is, I think, nothing which alarms fish so much as a shadow ; perhaps it is the fear of the unknown, for they are much more easily put off by shadows than when they see the fisherman himself.

Next we shall search the deep water behind Blackrock. Just before our first cast we notice that the crumbling sandstone of Blackrock is the nesting-place of pigeon. So we cast the plug (the darkest one we have) so that it appears to have dropped off the sheer face of Blackrock itself, and hope that perhaps Old Faithful will be deceived into thinking that it is a pigeon squab which has fallen out of its nest. Almost immediately there is a great swirl in the water and we are into this peer among fishes. At first his movement is unhurried ; he just cruises about in the deep water and we are unable to hold him or apparently make any effect on his movements whatever. Soon the constant pressure tells, and he bolts up into the white water where we can manage him better, so we let him go as far as the submerged rock. We have followed up the bank and are now at point X, from where we can apply side strain on the fish. To begin with it appears to have very little affect, but soon, by throwing him off his balance and making him fight the stream, he begins to give, and we get him just about opposite the corner of Blackrock. Here his resistance slackens, and he starts floating down stream on the current. This is serious, as, if allowed to continue he will go down the rapid where we can neither wade nor follow, so to wake him up we will throw in a boulder behind his tail. That shifted him, and it's straight up stream he has gone again. So much the better ; we can now go through the same tactics as before, only this time as he comes down he shoots round the corner of Blackrock and gets into deep water. Now that he is in slack water he will probably try to rub the hooks out on a rock or otherwise try and snag us. Soon we feel the telltale grating of the trace, and we must exert every ounce of strain we dare to keep him away from his pet snag. Again he goes floating downstream on the current, but this time on the far side, so that all hopes of turning him with a shrewdly flung stone are impossible. On the other hand we can apply side strain, so we lower the point of the rod and, braking the reel to locking point as the fish gives, instead of winding in, we walk backwards up the bank. Happily we bring him across to our own side, but we are not out of danger yet, so continue walking backwards upstream with the fish following. It is extraordinary how a fish can thus be marching upstream, whereas a single wind of the reel would irritate him and send him away with a rush. Having got our friend to point Y, we advance towards him and wind the reel. We have now got him near the shallows on our own bank, which is where we want him. His fight has now become dogged and sullen, but we continue to put as much pressure on him as we can, and, praise be ! get him well into the shallows. At last he is tired out. Calling for the gaff we get as close to him as we can, then, without any hurried movements, get the point of the gaff under him and drive it home in his lower jaw. Never try and gaff a large mahseer in the shoulder as his scales are very tough, and there is every chance of the point

❈ 57 ❈

not going home and the loss of the fish altogether in the flurry that follows.

Well, at long last here we have him, a great fish of thirty-five pounds, taken out of a very difficult pool in just the same time as you would have taken with the old-fashioned heavy tackle. We certainly had our terrifying moments, but no more than we would have had with heavy tackle. We have this advantage, however ; throughout the battle we have been in contact with the fish for every second, a contact which has allowed us to feel his every movement, almost at times to "feel" his very thoughts.

Again the scene changes ; this time we shall fish Tawi Pool, and what is more, fish it at various seasons of the year and at various times of the day. First, shall we say, on a warm morning in May, when the chilwa are running. We note that there are shallows on our bank and it will be up these that the fry will run, so we shall confine ourselves to casting along the bank. If the water is clear we might use a natural bait mounted on one of the mountings described in the previous chapter. If the water is slightly coloured I would advice the use of the River Runt Spook Silver Shore minnow. Actually I don't think there is anything to choose between a suitably coloured plug and natural bait. The plug is by far the cleanest and easiest to use, and of course, as it floats, you stand less chance of losing tackle on snags. Since the time is morning the fish are most likely to be in the streams and near the shallows ; if, on the other hand, we are fishing in the afternoon or evening I advise concentrating on the pool on the far bank and casting where the diagram shews a shoal of fish. On a warm day a shoal of mahseer will lie about in such a place from about three in the afternoon till well after sunset if the water is clear and gets the evening sun. What you hook is merely the luck of the draw ; it might be a fish of almost any size. The larger fish will lie deeper in the water than their small brethren, so adjust your bait accordingly. If you take a couple of fish quite early, let the pool have a rest, as when once a fish is hooked it is often followed about by the other fish of the shoal even whilst it is being played.

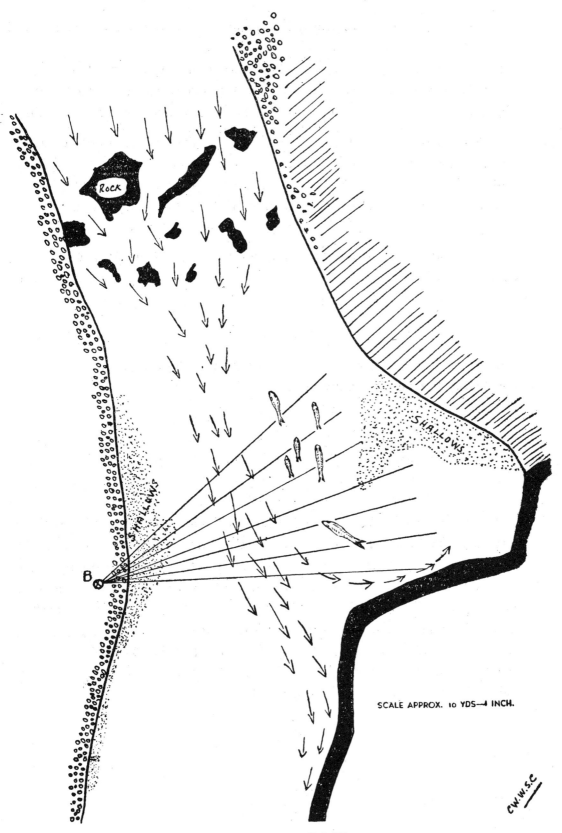

ROCK

SHALLOWS

S. SHALLOWS

B

SHALLOWS

SCALE APPROX. 10 YDS—1 INCH.

C.W.W.S.C.

Fig. II. TAWI POOL

Then after about an hour, or perhaps a little more, try again. It is peculiar the way mahseer will follow one of their number whilst it is being played this often gives an angler the idea that he has hooked two fish in one cast.

Now, should the water be dirty from a spate, I would advise casting right across the pool from point B or thereabouts, and letting the bait sink well before reeling in. In this instance use the Reflex Devon, as you will need to make the most of what light there is in the deep coloured water. For the shallows the long Norwegian spoon will be best.

I consider that perhaps the best conditions for Tawi Pool would be a break in the rains when the water has just had sufficient time to clear. Under these circumstances there is scarcely a place in the whole stretch of water under review which will not hold a feeding fish. Fish them all in turn ; first the shallows on your own bank, then the pool across the other side, next the slack water above it (probably with quite a good undertow), and finally the rapids themselves.

And now just a few words about the management of a bait in the water. In nearly every written work on fishing in India the advice given to the beginner is to cast across and downstream. You will have noticed that in the examples given above I have always advised casting upstream and a little across. Multiplying reels with their rapid powers of line recovery allow upstream spinning in all but what is virtually a waterfall ; let us therefore make the most of it. There will, on the other hand, be many occasions where upstream tactics are quite out of the question, as, for instance, where the stream runs through a narrow neck of high rocks and then opens out into a pool. Under such circumstances it might be worth while to float a plug down and retrieve it very slowly by means of pump handling the rod, so that the impression given is that of a small fish battling unsuccessfully against a strong current. Don't do this, however, if you are unable to follow down and play your fish in the pool below.

❊ 60 ❊

I have advocated bringing a plug down over sunken rocks and other snags. This may seem like madness to some fishers of the old school. But remember that the plug is a natural floater and that the depth at which it swims is regulated by the speed at which you recover it. Thus, if snagging is imminent, all you have to do is to slacken the speed of recovery and the plug will rise in the water and can be made to ride over the snag in which it would surely have otherwise got caught up. Again, if your plug is fast approaching a snag, a slackening of line followed by a quick backward jerk of the rod will often cause the plug to jump the snag.

In the examples given I have assumed that the fisherman is using the short rod. Plugs can, however, be fished with reasonable success with long rods and ordinary spinning reels. As you have seen, to catch fish with any great degree of success, accuracy and ease of casting are essential. This is easily obtainable with the short rod and gear I have described. The whole outfit comes to hand as though specially built for one. The moment the rod is gripped, the thumb takes up the correct position on the spool of the reel ready to give just that correct amount of brake so necessary for a good cast.

Though this book is written primarily for fishers who will follow the sport in hill streams, I feel that a few words on how to fish the many head-works of our Punjab canal systems will not be amiss. These canal head-works, situated as they are where the rivers leave the hills, offer the fisherman stationed in the plains the opportunity of a casual day's fishing.

The plan on the next page is typical of the layout of the head-works of a canal in the Punjab. It does not portray any particular place but claims to be typical of them all. In such place the fishing is probably at its best in the autumn, when the water has become clear, and there is enough of it to necessitate one of the bays on the main weir being open as well as at least one of the sluice gates. Below the sluices there is always a fine deep pool, the home of mulley, goonch and mahseer of all sizes. Above the

❊ 61 ❊

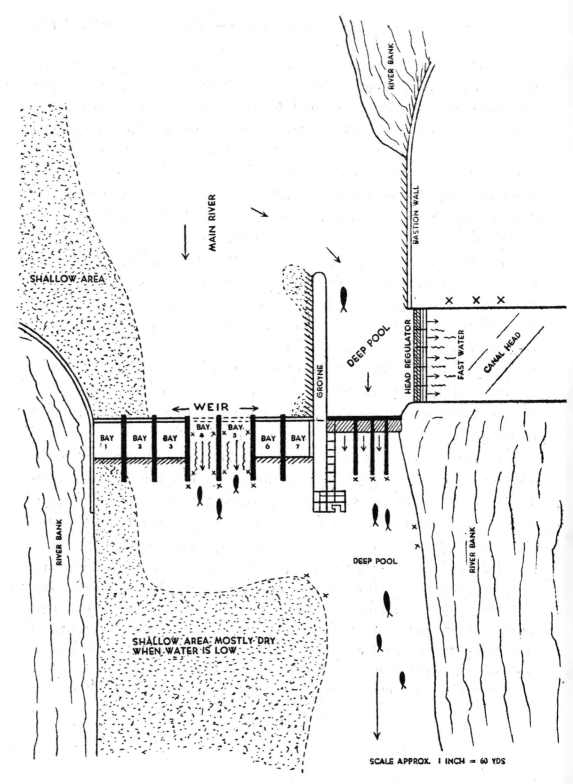

Fig. 12. TYPICAL CANAL HEADWORKS--PUNJAB

sluices there is a very deep pool which is usually the home of some mahseer of gargantuan proportions, but which are often very hard to come by. Large mahseer also tend to congregate in the rush of water below whichever bay of the weir happens to be open. (I have assumed that bays number 4 and 5 are open).

In any of these places a good all-round bait is the plug ; for patterns use the Pfleuger Pal-o'-Mine Perch markings and any of the lighter-coloured River Runt Spooks. Above and below the weir a large Norwegian spoon spun slowly will also kill occasionally.

Good fishing is often to be had in the spring and just before the snow water begins to come down. From the end of March until sometimes as late as the first fortnight of May the runs of chilwa occur. The presence of these small fish can always be detected by their leaping out of the water as their larger brethren prey on them. At such times I have found that a carefully mounted natural bait does most excellent execution.

If the area of river is one to which Butchwa run, good sport may be had with these excellent eating fish by spinning with the threadline and a natural bait mounted in a Scarab.

I have marked the best places to spin from with crosses in the plan ; of course local conditions may vary their position, but on the whole they give a very fair indication of where to start for anyone not acquainted with the particular place.

Whilst on the subject of fishing at canal headworks, I cannot let the opportunity pass of saying a few words regarding the fish ladders. Only this year I found two natives killing mahseer which were passing up a ladder, by the simple expedient of lifting them out in their loin-cloths ! It does seem to me to be such wasted effort to provide a ladder for the passage of fish, and then to do nothing towards ensuring the safety of the fish using it.

THE threadline outfit is so diverse in its uses that the fisherman using one should never be hard put to meet the peculiar requirements of the day and the fish. A word of warning, however ; the threadline is only meant for the smaller fish and should not be used for large mahseer. I have said that a dozen pounds' weight is the limit which one may consider tackling successfully, and no harm will be done by repetition of this statement. I have met many fishermen who, having used the threadline once or twice and having hooked a large fish on and suffered a bad break, condemn it out of hand. That large fish have been and will be killed on ultra-fine tackle is a fact not to be denied, but even then this is usually only done by men with considerable experience of its use. The threadline is comparable to the light fly rod used in conjunction with a fine cast, and should be used to take fish suitable for such gear. If your fishing is such that twenty and thirty pounders are your quarry you will most certainly require the heavier tackle represented by the short rod and the level wind multiplier. I am fully aware that there are on the market many threadline reels which are advertised as being capable of use with lines of a breaking strain of as much as fifteen pounds. With such heavy lines they are not, in my opinion satisfactory, and the beauty of the threadline – to wit, its very lightness – is completely lost. In the following pages I will refer to the taking of trout only in order to impress the above statements. For small mahseer in the hills the method of approach and the lies of the fish are the same as outlined in Chapter IV, thread-line tackle and suitable baits being substituted for those already described.

Plate VIII   "THREADLINE PRACTICE"

Many types of fishing may be undertaken, though I am sure that spinning will take premier place. The advantages of extremely light gear which may be cast a great distance are at no time more apparent than in the clear water which normally obtains in the Himalayan hill streams. All fish inhabiting the higher reaches of the hill sreams are very inclined to cannibalism ; perhaps it is the altitude, or perhaps the strength of the current requires that they should get more food with body to it. Furthermore, there is such a wealth of fry and tadpoles that the trout take naturally to them as a means of food. If we are to be successful, then, we should use baits which imitate these very small fry. In Chapter II, I have described the Scarab Tackle and the diminutive small metal devon minnow ; these are ideal baits for use with the threadline. I shall refer to them hereafter as "minnows," though minnows as one understands them in England do not exist in the Himalayan streams.

Besides fry, the trout feed on snails, fresh-water shrimps, the underwater larvae of various forms of insect, and last and by no means least the frog in its various stages.

Well, here we are on the banks of some mountain stream in the hills which has been stocked with trout for our delectation. The smell of wood smoke is in the air as it drifts from the wooden hut of a hill dweller. The waters of the stream are crystal clear and a low level, for the month is April and the melting snows have not yet had time to colour them. All around are the great hills, eerie in their majesty and still partly clothed in their winter coat of snow. Here the dark green of a pine forest seems to stretch up fingers which clutch at the snowfields ; there the white sheen of the snow has upon it a purple shadow thrown by a passing cloud. Spring is in the hills.

Today we have great hopes of tempting the unsophisticated appetite of some great golden trout who is on the look-out for small fry wherewith to satisfy his hunger. Hence we mount a one-inch gold or silver devon

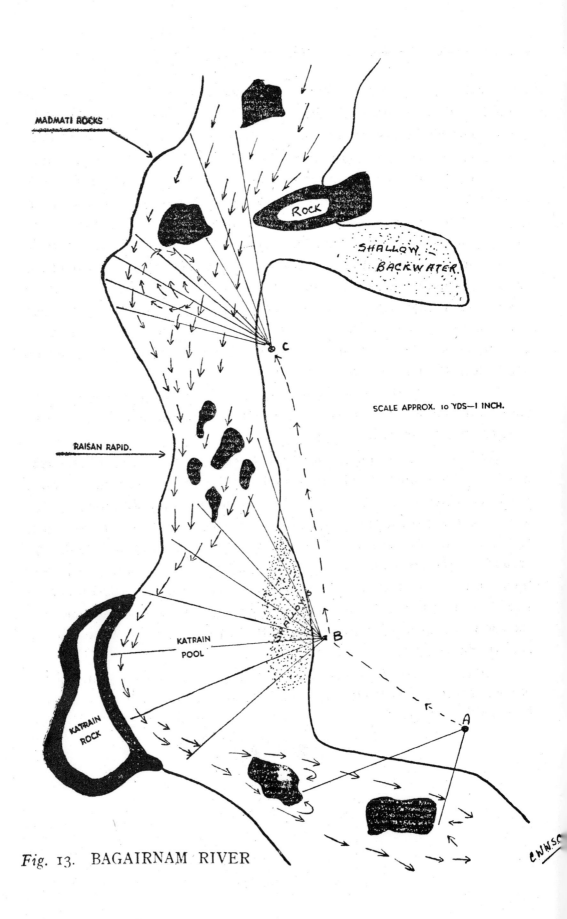

MADMATI ROCKS

ROCK

SHALLOW BACKWATER.

C

SCALE APPROX. 10 YDS—1 INCH.

RAISAN RAPID.

SHALLOWS

B

KATRAIN POOL

A

KATRAIN ROCK

Fig. 13. BAGAIRNAM RIVER

minnow, and, approaching the stream, study the water. We have in front of us the stretch of water portrayed in the diagram opposite (Fig. 13). Where will the fish we are after lie ? He is probably moving up from a deep pool to the shallower water where the fry he so much desires will abound. Near these shallows he will find for himself a lie where he can hide, to rush out and hunt down any poor unfortunate which seems at all disabled or approaches too near to make a quick get-away.

It is impossible to mention all such places, but the likeliest are sudden depressions in the channel, the edges of deep eddies, behind large stones, and where backwaters join the stream. All these are present in the water before us, and we are standing at point A. Immediately by us are two stones which stand out of the stream. Behind each of them is a backwash or eddy, shewn by the arrows. Our first cast will be to the downstream side of these rocks ; the backwash is strong enough to keep the light devon spinning for a minute or more before it loses way, so on completion of the cast we will allow the bait to hang in the stream, and then wind slowly in until the main current takes effect and forces us to increase the speed of the spin. The first cast produced nothing, so we will try again. This time there is a tug and we are into a nice fish of three-quarters of a pound which is duly netted. It is not worth while to expend more than two or three casts in such places, as if a fish will not take the bait by the third time of asking it is likely he will not be interested for some hours.

We now move to point B. Here we have a deep pool below a rapid, and at our feet some gravelly shallows. On the opposite bank there is Katrain Rock which has a smooth sheer face washed by the stream. The pool is obviously deep, and there is a good chance of it being occupied by a crafty old fish of noble proportions. He may be anywhere in the pool, so we adopt the system of radial casting in order that every inch of water may be searched. Nothing rewards us but a couple of fingerlings, hence we may safely assume that the big fish is not at home or is at least not moving today, as, if he were about, the little fellows would keep out of the way.

Raisan Rapid is too fast for spinning, as the bait would be forced out of the water with the strength of the current even if fished upstream, so we leave it alone and move to point C. Here we have a very interesting bit of water in front of us. Near the far bank we see a large stone which has behind it a minor whirlpool, and on our own bank a shallow backwater shielded by a large rock. Both of these places are just the lie which a large fish likes. Our first cast will be to the rear of the large stone on the far side of the stream. Again we will search the area out with radial casts. Then, as nothing rewarded our efforts, we will spin straight up just past the corner of the big rock which shields the backwater. What a tug! The strike on our part should be as near instantaneous as can be, and sufficiently vigorous to drive the needle-sharp hooks home. As this is obviously a large and healthy fish it will be some time before he is sighted, so we employ the immediate future in looking round for a suitable landing place. The fish in the meantime has rushed upstream for fifteen yards. We must be careful to keep a tight line on him and prevent him coming down again the wrong side of a rock, and so breaking us. As the fish is "swimming the current" and we are below him the odds are in our favour, and we should soon tire him. Now he comes downstream in a wild rush and throws himself out of the water as he turns. His downstream rush does not disconcert us, for we are able to keep the line taut owing to the rapid powers of recovery conferred on us by the four to one multiplication of the reel. Down he goes again, through Raisan Rapid and into Katrain Pool, and we follow down the bank, winding the handle of the reel forward when giving line but all the time keeping a taut line. Now his rushes are shorter and he shews signs of fatigue. Soon we can see him in the clear water, boring downwards and at times almost standing on his head. The fight will not last much longer, so we walk to a spot below the fish and by winding in bring him into the shallows at our feet. Even if he makes an unexpected rush when we are winding in, there is no fear of the line breaking, on account of the slipping action of the reel.

At last we have him playing on a line no longer than the length of the rod ; he is so exhausted that he is unable to strip off line against the clutch setting of the reel. We sink our landing-net in the water and bring the fish over it and then with a steady movement lift him out of the water. What a beauty – a cock fish of three pounds !

Let us assume that we are fishing the same stretch of water later in the year. We will now use the natural minnow in a Scarab mounting, for it is June and the fry which inhabit our stream have now grown larger. We will again spin the same places, but this time a little deeper, which is easily done with the extra weight contained in the body of the bait. Instead of bringing the bait back in a steady spin we bring it home by a succession of pulls and pauses, slowly in a gentle current and more quickly in a rapid one, *but never rapidly*. As the minnow passes a likely spot you may expect a rush at it, but if not go on spinning and, as the bait reaches the bank on your side, edge your minnow searchingly along the shore, helped at the last with a draw upstream with your rod. Many of the best fish are taken right under your own feet with this last movement, so do it very carefully. The secret of success in spinning of any sort is to imitate the action of an injured or frightened fish, thus to spin continuously or to drag the bait upstream in a steady long-drawn-out movement is only to warn your quarry, as no minnow will behave in such a manner. Make your bait appear to be striving unsuccessfully with the current, and sooner or later making for the safety of the bank or the shallows.

As the year progresses the thinnest water at the tails and edges of pools often give good sport, particularly in the early morning and at evening time, when predatory creatures such as old cannibals are well on the prowl.

Before leaving the subject of spinning for trout there are one or two points which are well worth remembering. First, regarding the hooking department ; the smaller the hooks the more certain the hooking ; and ensure that one hook at least lies just at the tail of the bait. Secondly, use the finest possible line commensurate with safety, and be careful to set the slipping clutch neither too lightly nor too strong.

Though spinning may be practised at all times of the year with a great deal of success, I have found that in the Himalayan streams it is at its best during the first half of the season ; and later, when the frogs come in, other baits such as plugs and large artificial "flies" of the lure type take the place of the baby devon and the natural minnow.

From July till the cold sets in, the frog abounds in the rice fields. They breed in the mud and shallow water which is heated by the sun. In the tadpole stage they are comparatively secure, unless a sudden spate sweeps them into a nearby stream to be gobbled up by a hungry and happy-hearted trout. The frog on reaching maturity starts his cross-country wanderings, and sooner or later hops into a stream, to meet the fate he escaped as a tadpole. It is a matter of constant surprise to me that frogs continue to exist in their millions in view of the numbers of fish, not to mention the various types of birds, which prey on them.

The best and most killing plug imitation of the frog I know is a Hardy-Jock Scott Wiggler, two inches in length, and the plug directions for the making of which are given in Chapter VII. In the case of the Hardy wiggler the best colour scheme is the blue and silver with a yellow stripe on the back. To fish the plug with success for trout the stiller water should be sought out, and as there is little current the most should be made of a long cast. Cast up and across stream, and fish the bait down at a pace just sufficient to keep it below the surface. Alternatively, having cast your plug up and across, it may be retrieved by a combination of reeling in and allowing the bait to float. To do this successfully calls for a nicety of judgement, as the plug should only be allowed to just reach the surface, and when travelling below water it should do so by a series of darts. The floating powers of the plug are often very useful, as the bait may be cast into a place full of known snags and manoeuvred into small patches of open water where it can be fished sub-surface.

Entrances to backwaters should always be given a trial, for backwaters are well-beloved of the frog. Overhanging grassy banks are another good place. Here your aim should be to make the plug represent a frog which, having hopped into the stream, is unsuccessfully striving to regain the safety of the bank.

For use with the small plug bait I advocate quickly-detachable double hooks of about size 8. Such double hooks have all the hooking properties of the treble, combined with the holding qualities of a single hook. Fine wire hooks of the utmost sharpness should always be used rather than any of a more robust construction, as the success of threadlining depends to a great extent on the ease with which the hooks may be driven home.

Lure fishing or as some will have it "wet fly" fishing, may be practised with great success with the threadline. The lure we shall use, though dressed like those used for sea trout at home, has this essential difference : it is leaded. By this I mean that lead wire is tied into the body of the fly when it is made. Lures may be of the one, two, or three hook variety ; thus they will always fall in with the rule of fly only, should such a rule obtain on the water of your choice. If it is your intention to use them in place of a spinning bait, a spinning head may be added. A spinning head consists of a bead with spinning vanes attached, revolving on a piece of single wire and attached to a link. They can be made by any "mistri" in the bazaar, and are a valuable addition to the tackle box.

The lures we shall use may be divided roughly into three classes *spinning lures*, *insect lures*, and the *bi-colour lure ;* in the last case the intention being to imitate the frog. To take them in the order given : first the spinning lure. These are the simplest, for they aim at nothing more than representing the natural fry, and when used with a spinning head are finished in the same manner and in the same places as the devon minnow or the natural small fish. The patterns I have found most successful for Himalayan trout are :– The Dandy Lure, the Coachman, Teal and Green, and the Jungle Lure. Of the insect lures we have the March Brown, which represents the grasshoppers which are to be found on the banks of the streams. Then the Alexandra, which gives a representation of a green-backed beetle which is often to be found in the vicinity of the streams and which is much relished by the trout. And last there is the Butcher, which also sets out to imitate the big black beetle found on the bark of trees growing by the waterside.

The insect lures are fished under overhanging foliage and near high banks. The great point to remember in using them is to fish them as slowly as you possibly can. Just allow them to swim in the stream from six inches to a foot below the surface. Other good places for insect lures are near large stones washed by the current and near over-hanging grassy banks. Long casting is quite unnecessary and I even venture to state militates against success. Some people seem never to acquire the knack of approaching a trout without disturbing it. Happily I have not suffered in this respect, and have on many occasions been able to approach to within four feet of a feeding fish without worrying him in the least. The fisherman has to vary his style of casting to suit the different kinds of water to be fished, and in like manner the length of his line. Usually ten to twenty feet of line is ample to fish most places on normal-sized streams when using the insect lure. Take, for example, a cast over a rough current to quieter water beyond, which we shall assume is shaded by low hanging branches. Here we shall cast out with a side flick, and in order to get the lure under the branches of the trees will lower the rod point almost to the water's edge. The rod point is then raised, leaving only a couple of feet of gut and the "fly" in the water, for if more of the line were allowed to become immersed the strong rush of the current which intervenes between us and the desired spot would act on it and pull our lure away. It is not easy to become an adept at placing the lure exactly where one wants it ; it is, however, very interesting fishing and the trout caught are normally much greater in size than with the straightforward fly. The secret of success is to approach the water carefully and not to frighten the trout ; to use a short line, and always to be in contact with the lure. Every offer from a fish should be responded to *at once ;* if too much line is in the stream, the fisherman has no knowledge of where his bait actually is ; a trout may have taken it and expelled it without any perceptible stoppage of the line or sense of contact with the man holding the rod.

And so we come to the Bi-Colour Lure. This sets out to imitate the smallest kind of frog. I mean the little fellow with a brown back and dirty white stomach. It is an all-hackle "fly" with two streamers of brown kid leather attached to its body about halfway down. The hackle are partridge for the first third of the body, then an "off-white" hackle for another third, and partridge hackle for the last third again. The kid leather streamers are attached in the part of the body covered by the off-white hackle feather. The armament of these flies is a large single hook and a small treble at the tail. The lead is all placed near this small tail treble, so that the "fly" will always sink by the tail when not actually being retrieved by the angler. Thus, if it is fished with a sink and draw movement the kid leather streamers will give a very good imitation of the kicking of the legs of a swimming frog.

To fish the "frog fly," use it with a sink and draw movement in the large pools. Never let the fly sink more than a foot or eighteen inches. The real frog seldom goes to any depth and spends a deal of time hanging in the water with but his head shewing, only diving and swimming when disturbed. Hence, when fishing the Bi-Colour Frog Lure (glorious name !) all you have to do is to think of the action of the natural frog ; if you can make your "fly" exactly imitate this, success is yours.   The frog lure is also very good in the "soda water" under and in the vicinity of small

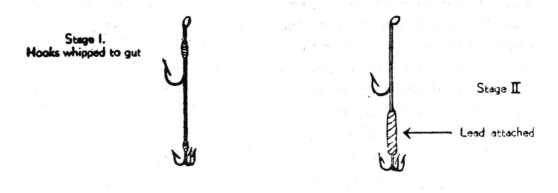

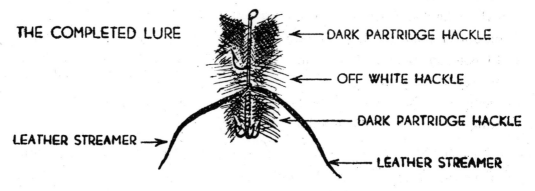

Fig. 14. FROG LURE

waterfalls of a foot or two in height which are constantly occurring in any Himalayan stream.   Yet another good place for their use is the very

❧ 74 ❧

white water of a rapid, particular care being taken as the "fly" emerges from the broken water into a pool. In all such places the sink and draw method is the only satisfactory way of managing the fly. Though it may sound rather unorthodox. I can assure you that the Frog Fly is killing in the extreme, but only when frogs are naturally there. It is quite useless in the reaches of streams which are away from the ricefields, for instance, where they run through rocky narrow valleys.

Full descriptions of how to tie all the lures mentioned above are given in Chapter VII of this book. I do most strongly advise any fisher to learn to tie his own flies ; it is not at all difficult and whiles away many an hour on a day when there is time to spare and fishing is a long long way off. Apart from trout, mahseer may be taken with these lures in small hill streams, the more particularly with the Frog Fly. There is withal a great satisfaction in catching fish on tackle of one's own making. The first attempts often look very comical and many a neophyte fly-dresser is discouraged by his first effort. A fly does not necessarily have to appear pretty to the human eye in order to take trout. Unscrupulous shops offer a huge variety of flies and lures and with them catch many more specimens of "homo piscator" than their flies will ever catch fish.

And now at long last we come to the taking of trout with the worm in clear water. There are many who decry the use of the worm as nothing short of downright poaching, and given conditions of flood water this may be true. Clear water worming for trout, and for mahseer too, is a sporting and skilful method of taking these fish. With the fly rod the difficulty has always been to keep the worm on the hook if a cast of any distance was to be made. With a threadline outfit, on the other hand, one may cast a worm as far as fifteen or twenty yards with ease and without fear of losing the worm.

Compared to spinning and fishing the lure, worming calls for greater dexterity, greater care in approach, and by far a greater knowledge of the haunts and habits of the fish.

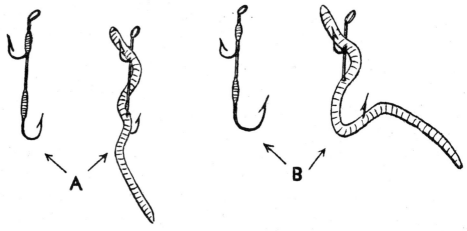

Fig. 15. WORM TACKLES

There are two essential tackles for use with the worm ; both are illustrated in figure 15. Type A is for use when fishing under normal conditions, and type B for use when the fish are shy or only tiddlers worry the bait. The hooks for type A tackle should be Size 12, and for type B the top hook should be size 12 and the lower hook size 5 with the top part of the shank nipped off. The tackle should be baited as shewn in the diagram. I tie my worm tackles with an eyed hook on top, so that they may be added or detached from a cast quickly. The distance between the hooks should be an inch, and the hooks themselves should be of the finest wire and very sharp. Hooks may be kept sharp by touching them up with a small file or carborundum slip every now and again. It is surprising how soon hooks of any kind will become blunter when in use in these fast rocky streams.

The cast for worming should not exceed a yard in length and may have a swivel of the smallest size at its junction with the reel line. This swivel adds considerably to the attractiveness and liveliness of the bait. A little lead wire may be wound round the cast about a foot to eighteen inches above the bait as circumstances require. Lead wire is in every way superior to split shot, as it does not catch in the rocks and other snags to the same extent. Many use stout gut for worming and also have their actual tackle tied on the very stoutest gut. This is a great mistake ; if you make it a rule never to use anything thicker than " 2x " gut you will not be far wrong, though for normal work I have found that 3x or 4x gut is quite strong enough even for big fish.

From June onwards, in waters where it is allowed, the worm is a deadly bait if fished properly, and the proficient will rely on it to produce the biggest fish of the trip. The first rule of successful worming is to fish always upstream. Secondly, the successful wormer is a man who has cultivated an "under water mind," and can read from the appearance of the stream's surface the lies and the whereabouts of the fish beneath. Provided the fisher can do both of these things, clear water worming may be compared to stalking only the best (and consequently the wariest) heads on the hill side. When worming, one does not go along the bank chucking in the worm indiscriminately and hoping to hook an unwary fish. Such a course only results in the loss of a great deal of tackle on the bottom and the capture of remarkably few sizeable trout, though quite a few fingerlings will come to hand. To worm a stream well considerable skill and method are required.

Well, here we are on the stream of our choice one September day. The water is nicely clear, as the rains are over and snow broth is no longer to be feared. We have a good supply of worms, which we carry in a flannel bag in which has been placed some damp moss and sand. We should aim to be on our fishing grounds at about 9 a.m., thus allowing the sun to get to the water and, in conjunction with the breeze that usually blows at that time of day, put the trout well on the feed.

We are again fishing the same stretch as portrayed in figure 13, but for a change, will fish it from the opposite bank. Again we start by casting behind the two large stones and allowing the worm to hang in the backwash. Next we approach the tail of Katrain Pool. Here the water shallows to a mere foot in depth. We must be very careful here to cast dead upstream in these shallows or we shall frighten the feeding fish. Wading is sometimes necessary in order to do this. But no hurried movement, or we shall cause the fish to bolt up into the pool and frighten all others there. We cast a long line and recover the bait slowly by winding the handle of the reel, so keeping contact, as the stream brings the worm down to us. Next we approach the foot of Katrain rock and cast well up into the current as its sweeps past it. The recovery of the worm here will have to be little faster owing to the speed of the stream as it sweeps past the face of the rock. We may have to add a little more lead in view of the depth of water. We must, however, avoid dragging the worm downstream ; our object should be to make it appear as though it were being carried down, suspended in the water. Katrain rock is too large to climb, as we walk round it and start fishing from the top end. Here our object will be to fish the quiet deep water between the stream and the shallows on the opposite bank. As the current is not so strong we will take some of the lead wire on the cast. Then casting up and across we allow the worm to sink, and, when we feel we have contact, draw it downstream or across with a sweep of the rod point. Now let the worm rest, move the rod forward again, and recover a little line by turning the handle of the reel. Then another sweep, and so on till the cast is fished out. Deep pools fished in this manner take quite a long time to exhaust and contain some of the largest fish. When worming, let your actions and methods be governed

DEDICATION

Plate IX   THE JUNGLE STREAM

by the principle of "Festina Lente"; at no time be hurried. It is more paying to fish a good stretch well than to cover many miles of water.

Above Katrain Pool we have Raisan Rapid. We again attach the lead wire we removed to fish the pool, as here the rush of water is very strong and we shall want to get the worm well down. We cast upstream into the current and keep contact with the returning bait by means of winding the handle of the reel. In order to feel any interference with the worm we will run the line over a finger and in fast waters strike immediately we feel a fish.

The strike is very easy as it consists of nothing more than tightening the line downstream. Most fishermen are far too rough. The needle-sharp wire hooks of a worm tackle take firm hold with the minimum force.

In pools or eddies a fish is often not felt when he takes. Here the fisher should watch the line and act when it is seen to stop or quiver. I have found it an advantage to finish all casts in water of this description with a gentle draw downstream, the rod top being lowered before the final sweep is given. In so doing many a fish is hooked which would otherwise have been only touched, as they often take the worm as it is being lifted out of the water, which prevents an affective strike by the fisherman.

Above the rapid we have Madmati Rocks and the entrance to the little backwater. These should be fished as already described Other good places where trout may be confidently expected with the worm are runs beneath an overhanging bank, the roots of trees washed by the current, and where the shallows merge into deeper water. Finally, no eddy or corner in the vicinity of large stones should ever be passed over, no matter how shallow.

Chapter VI

BAIT FISHING

A GREAT number of fishermen, particularly. if they are fly purists, regard all forms of bait fishing as anathema. So let us start right at the beginning with the idea that bait fishing is by no manner of means to be despised as anything unsporting. It is every whit as difficult to be a master with the float as to be the king of dry fly experts.

Bait fishing usually brings to the mind the picture of a seedy, down-at-mouth individual, sitting on the banks of some stream asleep, with a float in the water, an empty beer-bottle beside him, and not a care as to whether a fish should take the bait or not. Such a fisherman has become a butt of the low comedian together with the mother-in-law of the music halls. Well, as we have started with this talk of floats, let me discuss them from the point of view of the bait-fisher proper. I have no knowledge of tank fishing in India, so my remarks will be directed to the use of the float as a means of catching fish in streams and rivers.

There are three main purposes which a float fulfils. First, it maintains a baited hook at a predetermined level below the surface of the water. Secondly, it indicates to the angler any interference of any sort whatever with the bait. Thirdly, it is a means whereby a baited hook can be taken to any part of the water which the angler cannot reach by means of casting or in circumstances where wading would frighten the feeding fish. Thus, the float opens up a wide range of possibility to the fisherman who is prevented from using spinning tackle or the plug. I personally do not use bait tactics unless all else fail, as I consider that spinning is by so much the more pleasant way of taking fish than with bait. Be that as it may, there are many days in the fishing year when bait, and bait only, will kill a fish, and so turn an otherwise unsuccessful day into one that at least you will not regret.

There are all sorts and varieties of floats. Round ones, cigar-shaped ones, egg-shaped ones, single quills, and a host more. As the duty of the float is to keep the bait suspended in the water, we do not want anything with a greater buoyancy factor than the minimum required to do this; for, with a big buoyancy factor, more weight is required to make the float cock and it is not nearly so sensitive. Again, the float, on being pulled under water, will displace its own weight of water, so that the fish will have quite a noticeable tug on his mouth before the fact of his presence is communicated to the fisherman on the bank. In the case of the average round float, shown as 'A' in Figure 16 the maximum surface is offered to the water when the fish takes. If, on the other hand, the cigar-shaped float is used the cork part is tapered and the displacement is gradual and so the fish does not feel it all at once. (In short, the elements of streamlining arise). But to return to this question of the displacement of water. If the cast is so shotted or weighted that the tip only of the float shews above the water, the displacement is very slight when the fish takes, as there is really nothing more than the thickness of the quill to go under. Thus, if we always use the float shewn in diagram B, and so weight the cast that only the tip is above water, we shall have a float which is very sensitive, and which will give us the warning we so much desire when there is the very least interference with the baited hook.

Another of the main purposes of the float was to keep the bait at a predetermined level below the surface of the water. On the face of it, that appears easy – just a matter of putting on sufficient shot and adjusting the length of the cast under water. But, if you stop to think, there is more in it than that. If the surface of the water has any small waves on it the float will go bobbing along and the bait underneath will do the same. Now, all fish who have lived a sufficient time to become takeable are aware that

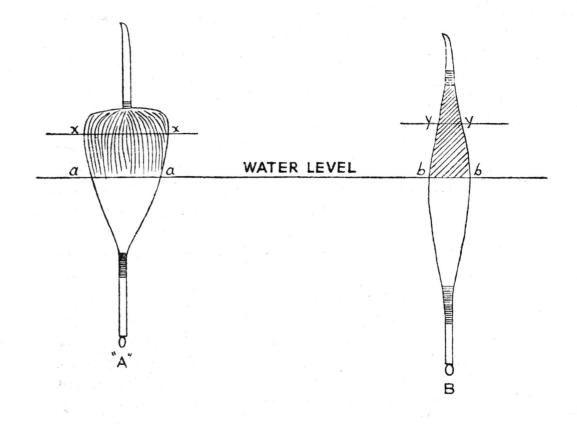

WATER LEVEL

"A"

B

FLOAT "A."
As the float goes under the water, the area of resistance
offered to the water INCREASES, and the diameter of
float become " X—X "

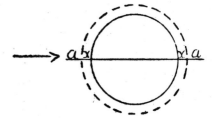

FLOAT "B"
As the float goes under the water the area of resistance
offered to the water DECREASES, and the diameter of
the float becomes "Y—Y"

Fig. 16. DISPLACEMENT OF FLOATS

no toothsome morsel will go jumping about under water with a regular cadence. Therefore our problem is to contrive to keep the bait travelling on a level keel. This is done by cutting down the buoyancy factor of the float so that it is not affected by the surface waves and ripples. If the float has half its body sticking out of the water its buoyancy is at its greatest. Hence, we shall shot it down until only the tip is above water.

So far so good, but I am sure that the first question you will ask is : how on earth am I going to keep the tip of the float in view ? it is a small enough object in all conscience. Well, that is easily overcome by tying to the top of the float a feather. The colour of this feather must be chosen with due regard to the colour of the water and the light conditions. A white feather in slightly coloured water shews up very well. In clear water a red feather leaves little to be desired.

The last of the main purposes of the float was to take the bait to such places as could not be reached by casting, and where wading was impossible or undesirable. I mentioned that wading might frighten the feeding fish. If we are going to all this trouble not to frighten fish, let us for a moment consider the colouring of the float itself. So many that are sold have the most weird and marvellous colouring. For instance, one I saw in the tackle box of a friend of mine a few days ago had a green top and a red underneath. Now, can you bring to mind a single thing at the water-side that has a red underneath ? No, I am sure you can't. Well, the fish down there in the stream have that much intelligence too, and when they see some great flash of red above them they will take no further interest in your baited hook until they have investigated what it is. As regards the green top I have nothing to say but that it is probably the most difficult colour to keep in view once you have made a cast.

Look at the next fish you catch and you will see that it is white underneath. God made fish like that so that they would be as near invisible as possible to any creatures below them. Paint your float accordingly and you will be safe, at any rate, from frightening the fish in the water with it.

We have spoken of the important matter of shotting or weighing the cast, so a few words on the best way of doing this will not be amiss. Split shot is not the best form of weight to use ; in fact, I think that for nearly all forms of fishing, shot of any sort is definitely bad. Shot have a wonderful habit of catching in all manner of underwater snags. The best ways of leading your cast are illustrated in figure 17. I place the use of lead

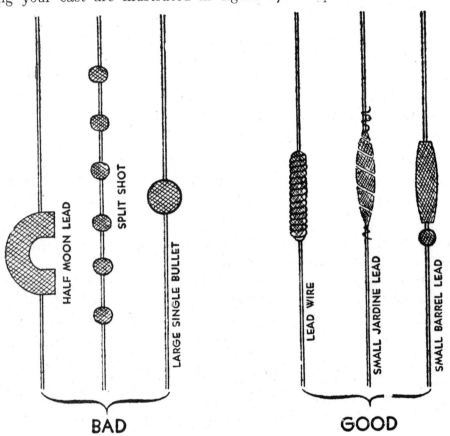

Fig. 17. · SHOTTING THE CAST FOR BAIT FISHING

wire first ; it can be adjusted to suit special needs and its pliability, even when mounted, helps a lot in preventing snagging. Next I think the use of the smallest sizes of Jardine leads take a lot of beating. They are easily detachable and don't get snagged too much; they have, however, the disadvantage of not allowing the finer adjustments of weight. Lastly, the barrel lead, mounted as shewn in the diagram, are quite good, but suffer from the same disadvantages as the Jardine lead.

For casts, the use of gut substitute cannot be bettered for Indian conditions. I never use a cast of more than a yard and a half in length. The strength of the cast and the size of the hooks will, of course, depend on the size of fish you intend or hope to take. Personally, I do not think that anything thicker than a seven-pound breaking strain is ever warranted. The knots to use and the method of binding on hooks are given in Chapter VII, so we will not waste time on them here.

As regards the hooks, it is difficult to lay down a standard size, as much depends on the condition of the water. For clear water I use an Alcock's Model Perfect No. 5 size for atta. The paste is put on as shewn in figure 18. If the water is coloured I am inclined to use a smallish

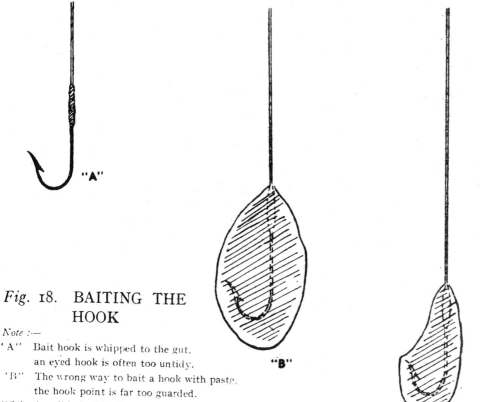

Fig. 18. BAITING THE
         HOOK

Note :—
'A' Bait hook is whipped to the gut, an eyed hook is often too untidy.
'B' The wrong way to bait a hook with paste, the hook point is far too guarded.
"C" A well baited hook—*cf.* fishing with "atta"

treble hook (a size 7 will do) and cover it with *atta*. It is amazing how *atta* accounts for many of the biggest fish. So be careful ; the take is often very gentle and belies the size of the fish responsible.

Many other forms of bait may be used : worms, goat's liver, meat, large grasshoppers, and a host of others. Whatever bait you intend to use, adjust your cast so that the bait is about a foot off the bottom of the stream. This appears to be where the mahseer appreciate it most, and it also saves hang-ups and loss of tackle which would occur if the bait is too near the bottom. If the bait is higher than a foot from the bottom of the river bed the fish are very inclined to give it the go-by. When bait fishing it is always worth while to throw some *atta* flour into the water at the top of the run. In this state it travels downstream in a nebulous but appetising cloud, and brings fish on the feed. Then, as you cast your float in, throw one or two pellets of *atta* paste generally about the area you intend your bait to travel.

I find that the addition of a little finely-grated cheese will often tickle the appetite of the fish. Honey helps to keep the *atta* paste on the hook in fast water if it is mixed with the paste.

Using a float, the bait can be made to travel to almost any spot by means of moving the rod top and tightening or giving line. When you see what is probably a good lie, manoeuvre your bait there. There is a great deal of skill in thus causing your bait to swim in just the places you intend. Expertness in the control of a moving float is only achieved after considerable practice. When using bait, fish in much the same places as for spinning. The big deep pools where water is very still are not much good. They unquestionably hold some fine fish, but they are not nearly so amusing to fish.

I find that after two or three fish have been killed from any one stance it is best to move on, owing to the peculiar habit of the mahseer in following any one of their comrades who have been hooked, almost to the bitter end.

Come back later and try again if you like, but the longer you rest the pool after killing a few from it the better are your chances of sport next time.

Many fishermen will groundbait a place beforehand. I consider that this is very seldom necessary. The number of fish in the average Indian stream is so much greater than at home, that to me ground-baiting savours of being a little unsporting.

The short rod is not normally suitable for fishing with the float, owing to difficulty in casting if the length of gut cast below the float is over a couple of feet. Yet another drawback is that a sufficiently light strike is not easily attainable. Float fishing may be practised with great success with the threadline and also with the level wind multiplier mounted on a country ringall cane.

For bait fishing with *atta* paste, etc., I cannot too strongly advocate the use of hooks whipped to the gut and not eyed hooks. The fish has every opportunity of examining the bait offered to him, hence one does not wish to draw his attention to the gut cast on account of an unsightly knot at the head of the hook. The method of whipping hooks to gut is given in Chapter VII, and it is well worth the while of any fisherman to master it, thus enabling him to make up tackle at the waterside which is both neat and serviceable.

It is not always necessary to use a float for bait fishing. A hook baited with a pellet of *atta* may be cast into runs, and the fish struck when the line is seen to tauten. Threadline is ideal for this type of fishing. The fish are brought well on the feed by throwing in pellets of *atta* paste at the head of a run or rapid. Then, after a pause, cast in the baited hook and let the current carry it down. Feeding fish can often be seen poised in the stream ; the fisherman gets great satisfaction in casting to an individual fish.

If in the river of your choice the fish are known to be partial to any particular form of bait, always try and use it. Sometimes these baits are strange, and often the last thing that you would consider using. In support of this I quote the experience of a friend of mine who was fishing from his houseboat at Ganderbal (Kashmir). After bottom fishing with a variety of bait, including worm, atta and meat, he was advised by a local shikari to try curried spinach ! Apparently this is the staple dish of the houseboat "mangys," and (as the leavings of their meals go overboard) also of the fish. His method of mounting the curried spinach on the hook is so ingenious that I feel it is worth mention, especially as many of my readers will no doubt be fishing in Kashmir sooner or later.

A piece of cotton some three inches long is tied to the shank of a single hook ; a piece of spinach is then wrapped round the hook from the shank downwards and bound lightly with the cotton to prevent it being washed away. No weights or float are necessary. Cast into a pool close to the stem of a houseboat near the bank, cast out the baited hook and hold the line lightly between finger and thumb. The line will transmit the nibbles of the fish, then strike lightly, and you are well in to a choosh. My friend informs me that he has taken a goodly number of choosh of about two pounds in weight in this manner, and, what is more, never had a blank day.

Another of my friends swears by a piece of *chapatti* as a bait for mahseer in the Jhelum river. His method of fishing is as follows : He takes a piece of *chapatti* about an inch square and impales it on a size 5 hook. This he casts into backwaters and eddies and plays it about on top of the water, the mahseer rising to the *chapatti* like trout to a dry fly. He kills quite a few fish in this way every year, and has become a veritable magician at working the piece of *chapatti* on the surface of the waters without drag.

The worm is a good bait for mahseer in the rains and in coloured water. It does not normally attract the attention of the largest fish, but very pretty sport may be had with it on the sides of heavy runs when the chances of using the plug or a spinning bait are poor. I have caught a number of fish other than mahseer with the worm in the falls that occur here and there in the Punjab canal systems, particularly during the rains. Most fish will take a worm, if on the feed, with complete confidence, but the manner in which they all do it is worthy of notice. For some reason I have never been able to fathom, fish have a dislike of swallowing a worm other than lengthwise. They almost invariably take the worm across the middle and then turn it round in their mouths. In order to ensure that a good hook hold is obtained, use the two hook tackle described in Chapter V I do not advocate the use of the large single hook. To get the best from worm fishing, the worm should look natural on the hook and be lively This is only possible if, when mounting the worm, it is punctured as little as possible. With the large single hook the only way to mount the worm is to thread it on to the hook for half its length, and so successfully killing it.

As mahseer live on the whole in streams with rocky or stony beds, the use of the ledger normally results in the loss of very much tackle, and is a sore trial to patience. Hence I cannot advocate it for general use. Where, however, you know the bed of stream to be sandy or otherwise clear of snags, it may be used to advantage. A simple ledger tackle is shewn in figure 19. The ledger is cast out and left till a fish takes it. The rod may be held by hand or rested against a stone, when sundry quiverings and shakings of the rod top will advise the fisherman of the presence of a fish. Ledgering is not a very exciting form of fishing, but it has its uses during the lunch interval or afternoon siesta.

The ledger may be baited with almost any bait :—*atta* paste, liver, minnow, worm or prawn are all good. It is essential that the bait is one which will stay on the hook well, as both small fish and river prawns, as well as divers other creatures, are very apt to interfere with the bait on the hook.

Fishing the Prawn. Fishing the prawn is very little practised in India, which is indeed a matter for surprise, as the prawn is perhaps the most

L

deadly of all baits for mahseer when presented to him in the right place. Most Indian rivers abound in prawns. They are the scavengers of the river bed. A certain lady of my acquaintance was horrified when I shewed her a dead dog that had been under water for a long time and all over the body was a seething mass of fresh-water prawns. A little earlier in the day she had been extolling to me the virtue of the river prawn for table use! The trouble about prawns as bait is the fact that, as sold in the bazaar, they always have the head and "legs" removed. In this state the prawn is useless. After a little gentle (*sic*) persuasion your cook will,

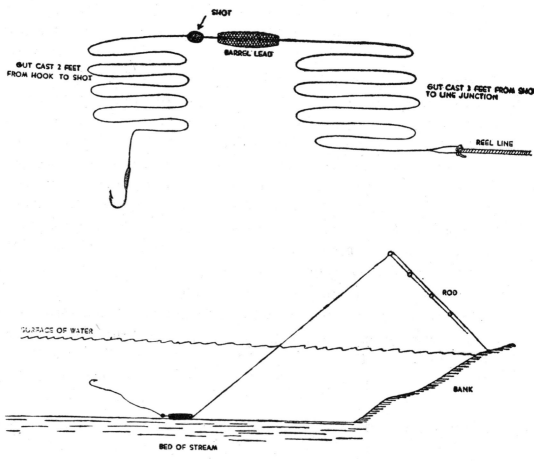

Fig. 19. THE LEDGER

however, be able to produce the necessary prawns from the bazaar without any difficulty, although at first he will assure you that only the best Karachi prawns (and consequently headless) are available.

The prawn may be fished either fresh as it is caught, or slightly boiled, when they get a pale shrimp pink colour. In either state they are equally attractive to the fish. This matter of boiling prawns must not be overdone. They only need plunging into boiling water until the colour turns, otherwise they become too soft and cannot be mounted properly for fishing. If the water is very clear perhaps the odds are in your favour if the prawn is fished in his natural colour, but if there is the slightest suspicion of colour the prawn may be boiled. Whether boiled or not, always make a point of using them as fresh as you possibly can.

The mounting for prawns is very easily made. Two treble hooks are lashed to a loop of strong gut or gimp about three inches in length. Now take a piece of wire (a straightened paper clip will do) and with the aid of pliers cut it to a length of about two and a half inches. File one end to a point and bend the other into a small eye big enough to take the loop of gut. Now round the gut near the hooks wrap some lead wire and colour it with some red enamel. Your prawn tackle is complete. Take your prawn and, handling it very carefully, skewer it on the wire so that it becomes straightened out. Lay the hooks along its tummy and bind the whole with some fine soft copper wire. A glance at the diagram (fig. 20) will make it quite clear. Loop the gut end on to a swivel and attach to your trace.

It is worth while mounting some half-dozen prawns like this before you go to the water's edge and putting them in a tin.

The best places for using prawn are in pools near a village ; here the prawns collect in large numbers and the mahseer need no second invitation to take. Unfortunately, many of these village pools are sacred, and as

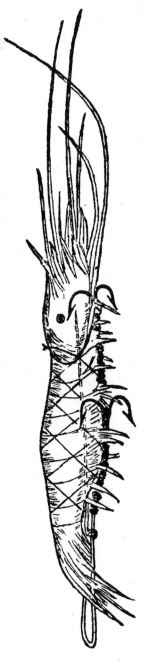

The mounted Prawn, mounted on the skewer and with the hooks
bound on with fine mounting wire

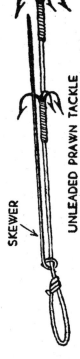

SKEWER

UNLEADED PRAWN TACKLE

SKEWER

LEADED PRAWN TACKLE

Fig. 20. PRAWN TACKLE

such should never be fished by a sportsman. Apart from the question of offending the religious susceptibilities of the locals, these sacred pools are natural fish sanctuaries and do a great deal of good in keeping up the stock of fish in the river. The fish in sacred pools are also very tame, and the idea of killing them is unsporting. Where, however, the pool near a village is not sacred it should be tried out with the prawn in preference to anything else.

Your first cast should be into the head of the pool and at an angle of about forty-five degrees to the stream. Don't wind in a hurry : let the prawn play about in the current ; the deeper it gets the better. Then very slowly retrieve it when the stream brings it round to your own bank. If there is a bag in the line raise your rod point until you have control again. It is essential that you keep contact with the prawn or you will surely lose many of your tackles. The secret of successful prawn fishing is not to be in a hurry. If you think a fish has taken don't strike as it is probably only a snag. When a fish does take he does so in no mean manner, and there will not be the slightest doubt in your mind as to what has happened. The mahseer takes the prawn with the most astonishing abandonment, with the result that the hook hold is usually well down in the throat.

The trace for prawn fishing should be a little longer than that for spinning ; the fish have a greater time to look at it. Many of the prawn tackles on sale are in the form of spinners. Leave them all alone. Spinning the prawn may be all right for salmon at home, but the mahseer like them to move very slowly. The art of prawn fishing lies in keeping the bait just moving and off the bottom, and no more.

To close this chapter on bait fishing I write of a form of float tackle invented by Mr. Alexander Wanless, of Threadline fame, and described in his book "*The Modern Practical Angler*" (op. cit. page 143). As this method of fishing is so entirely suitable to India, I will describe it and its various modifications in some detail, at the risk of being accused of plagiarism.

The tackle consists of a cork, through the centre of which is inserted a short celluloid tube, through which the line is threaded. The gut cast should be about a yard in length and the line well dressed so that it floats. To the cast is knotted a "stop" about eighteen inches above the hook ; and the float is free to move up and down the line and cast. The tube also lessens the resistance of the float when a fish takes the bait. We have thus

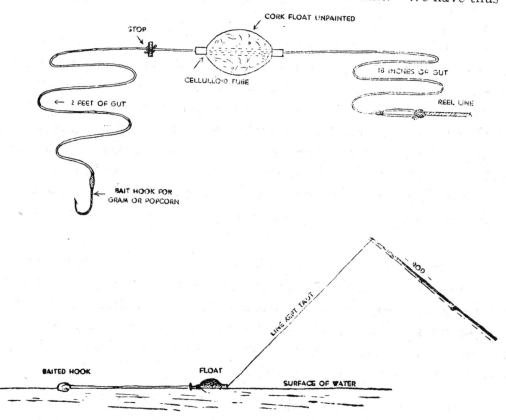

TACKLE IN USE

Fig. 21. FLOATING LEDGER

a "floating ledger" tackle ; sufficient weight in the float to make casting a reasonable distance possible, and yet an entirely unweighted bait which is able to move about absolutely unencumbered.   Figure 21 shews the tackle ready for action.

Many types of bait may be used ; perhaps the most successful for mahseer in full streams is the large grasshopper which is found in the grass on the banks.   This should be captured by hand and damaged as little as possible.   (Any village urchin will collect them in considerable numbers for you for a small monetary consideration).   The grasshopper may be mounted on a largish two hook Thomson tackle (hooks about size 10). The top hook is inserted through the belly of the bait and the tail hook through the thorax.   The grasshopper itself should be damaged as little as possible, as the livelier it is, and the more commotion it makes on the surface of the water, the greater are your chances of success.   The baited tackle is cast out and allowed to float down with the stream, and though the float should be kept up against the stop, no drag should occur on the bait.   This certainly calls for a nicety of touch, which is soon picked up after one or two trials.   Alternatively, one of Alcock's Ayrbro hooks may be used for baiting with the grasshopper.   These Ayrbro hooks are mounted with a little spring catch which securely holds the bait without it having to be impaled on a hook in any way.   When a fish takes, it should be allowed plenty of time to get the bait well into its mouth.   Fishing the natural insect in this manner is very exciting, as the take is visible and occurs more often than not with just a suck and an ominous "bulge" in the water.   The tackle may be used with either the threadline, or the level wind multiplier with either the short or the long rod.   It is at its best with the threadline, however.

To the fisherman in India who goes in for gram and popcorn fishing, I feel that this tackle will come as a boon and a blessing, the main difficulty of using popcorn or gram being that of keeping it on the hook and of

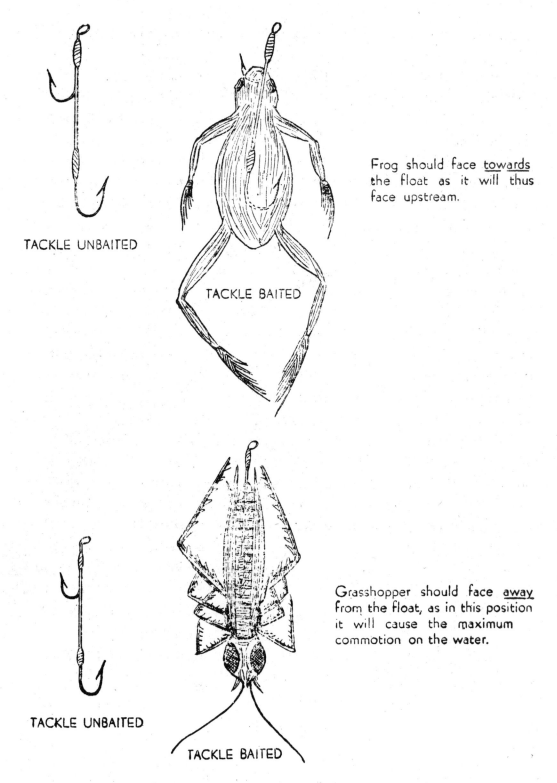

TACKLE UNBAITED

TACKLE BAITED

Frog should face <u>towards</u> the float as it will thus face upstream.

Grasshopper should face <u>away</u> from the float, as in this position it will cause the maximum commotion on the water.

TACKLE UNBAITED

TACKLE BAITED

Fig. 22.   TACKLES FOR USE WITH THE GRASSHOPPER & FROG

Plate X

THE GAFF STROKE

preventing it sinking down into the depths. When using this method the most it can sink is a mere foot or so, and is thus always well placed for feeding fish which are in midwater. When fishing with popcorn and gram it is advisable to bring the fish on the feed by throwing in a few handfuls of bait at the top of the run. Then, after a pause, and when the fish are rising nicely, down goes the baited hook. The angler should remain out of sight as much as possible, and when he has killed two or three fish from a stance move on to another run. In this method the fishing is *downstream* and therefore the necessity of keeping out of sight cannot be overstressed.

By increasing the size of the float a very deadly live bait tackle for use with the frog is obtained. Smallish frogs are best ; and note that they must be frogs and not toads. The frog should, of course, be fished alive ; it does not matter whether it is on the surface or just under it. What is important is that the frog should not be dragged about in any way but as far as possible should have complete freedom of movement. To mount the frog, use a two hook tackle as for the grasshopper, only the hooks should be about size 5 for a frog and one and a half inches in length, with the hooks tied an inch apart. Put the top hook through the lips of the frog and the tail hook through the skin of his back.

Apart from the above, and that very rarely, I seldom use live bait in any shape or form myself. It savours of being a little unsporting, and I have not found it more killing than any of the other ways of taking fish that I have described.

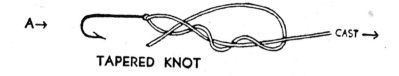

TAPERED KNOT

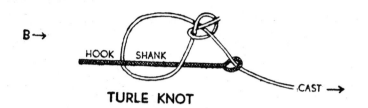

TURLE KNOT

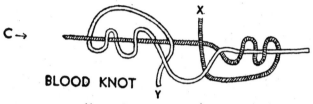

BLOOD KNOT

Note: Pull tight and clip off spare ends X & Y—Right hand length of gut clear—Left hand length shaded.

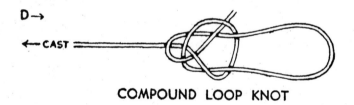

COMPOUND LOOP KNOT

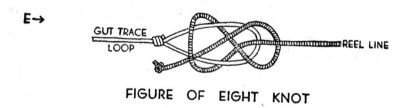

FIGURE OF EIGHT KNOT

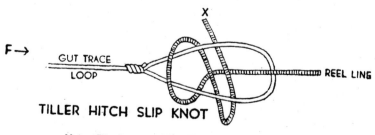

TILLER HITCH SLIP KNOT

Note : The knot may be slipped by a pull on X.

Fig. 23. KNOTS

Chapter VII

MAKING, MENDING, & Other Oddments

ONE of the most important matters to do with fishing is knot-tying. An old adage states that the strength of a chain lies in its weakest link. The same applies to fishing tackle. A break and a lost fish resulting from a bad knot drives one into a fury such as no break from honest-to-goodness snagging will do. Hence, I make no apology for including a list of knots which have been tried by generations of fishermen the world over and have not been found wanting.

Starting from the hook, we have two methods of attaching an eyed hook to gut. When using gut substitute it is always worth while to make doubly certain of a knot by finishing it off with a dab of that excellent commodity " Rawlplug Durofix," a tube of which should always find a place in the tackle box. Two knots shown opposite are (A) the Tapered knot, and (B) the Turle knot. Both are equally good.

Having attached our hook to gut, we want to join together two lengths of gut or gut substitute ; for this purpose there is the Blood knot, which is in a class by itself. (Figure 23, C.) When using gut substitute another means of preventing a knot drawing or slipping is to lay a piece of soft bait mounting wire alongside one of the strands of gut substitute and to tie it in with the knot.

The next requirement we shall have is to make a gut loop at the top end of the trace or cast for easy attachment to the reel line. For this purpose I recommend the compound knot (see Figure 23, D).

And finally, having made up our cast or trace, we will wish for a reliable knot wherewith to attach it to the line. A choice of two is available. First the figure of eight knot for use with ordinary lines. In this case the end of the line should itself be knotted to prevent it drawing under strain. For use with the threadline or with any other very fine line I advocate the Tiller Hitch (see Figure 23, F). The Tiller Hitch has the great advantage of being easily undone when baits have to be changed frequently.

When making up spinning traces we shall want a good strong method of attaching the gut substitute to the eye of the swivel. Furthermore, as

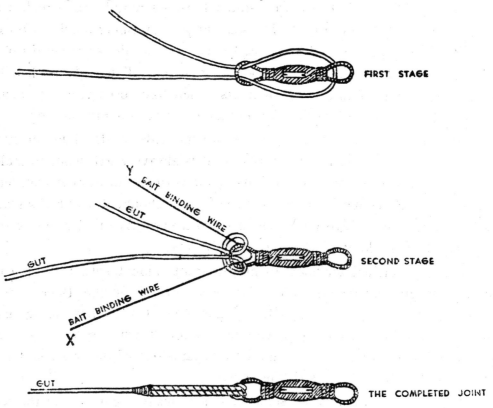

Fig. 24. FASTENING GUT TO A SWIVEL WITH BAIT BINDING WIRE

wear is quite considerable at such a point, we shall also want the knot reinforced. What could be better than the soft bait binding wire which we have in our tackle box for this purpose ?

Double the end of the gut substitute, passing it through the eye and over the swivel. Now take some four or five inches of wire, put it through the eye of the swivel, and adjust it so that the end of the wire and the short end of the gut are the same length. We shall now have a long and a short end of wire (x and y in Figure 24). Twist the wire and gut substitute together and finish off the whole by winding the long end of the wire round the two strands of gut substitute and the short end of the wire some half-dozen turns. The whole joint should occupy a length of about three-quarters of an inch, and is very neat and invisible in the water.

The foregoing knots are shewn clearly in the diagrams in black and white, and if the knots are practised with different coloured pieces of string against a suitable background, there should be no difficulty in learning them with a little practice. It is of inestimable value to be able to tie good knots without having to look too closely at what one is doing, as sooner or later it will have to be done in bad light or in darkness.

Leaving gut, we come to killin wire, which we shall use a great deal for traces. Wire should *at no time* be attached directly either to a line or to gut. Invariably effect the junction with a swivel ; killin wire is very sharp and will sooner or later cut through gut or line under strain. Agreeing on this, we therefore require only a means of attaching a length of wire to the eye of a swivel. The best way of achieving this is shewn in figure 25. Care should be taken that at first *both* strands of wire are evenly twisted round each other for at least a quarter of an inch, and then, to finish off, the shorter end is wound round the trace proper. Clip off the spare piece *short* against the trace, and the joint is complete. It is important not to have the spare end standing out in any way, as it will surely catch up any weeds which may be about. Many anglers solder the binding to prevent this. Personally I have found it to be an unnecessary refinement. But for those who wish to do so, I strongly recommend the use of Brittinol, which is a soft solder applicable without an iron and with only the heat of a match.

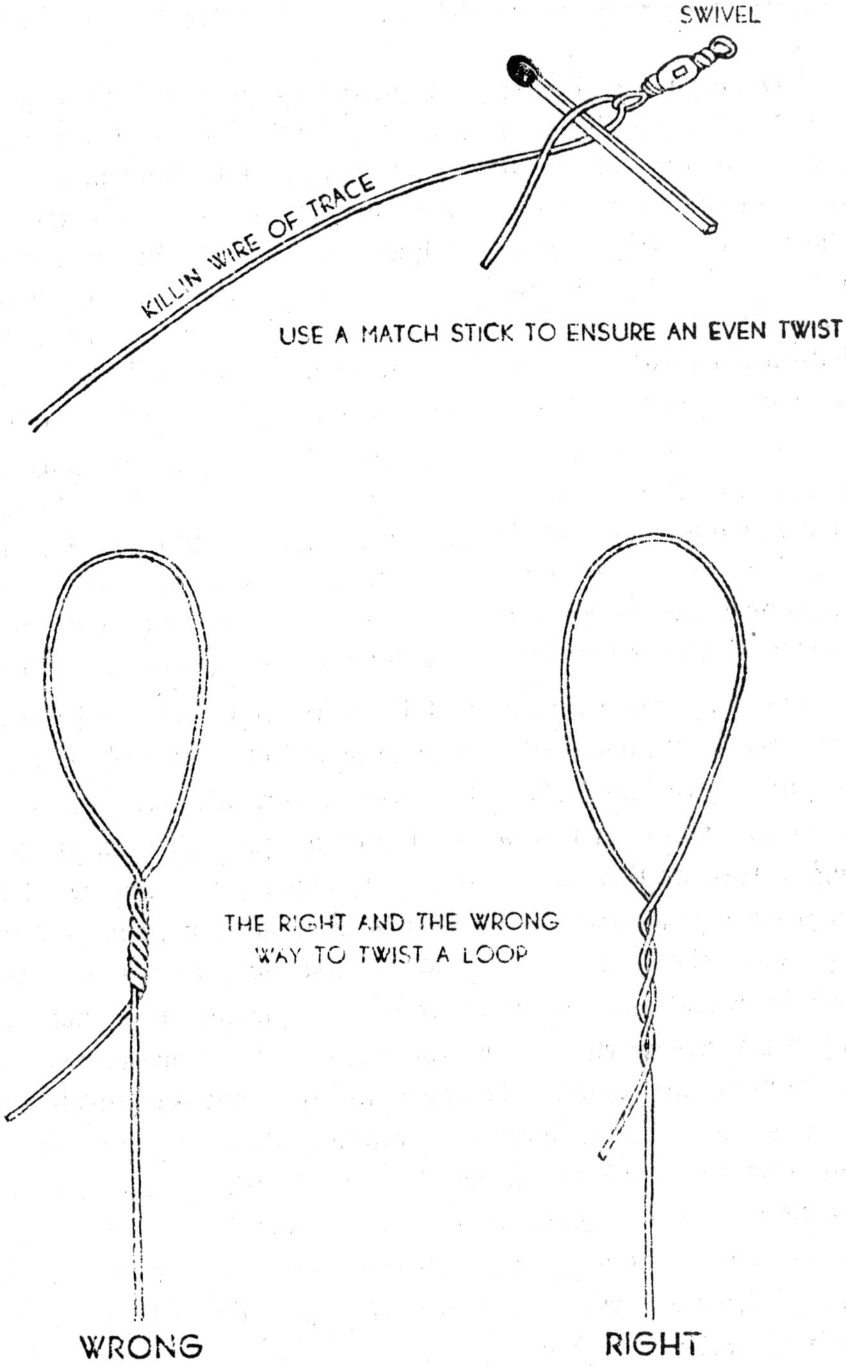

SWIVEL

KILLIN WIRE OF TRACE

USE A MATCH STICK TO ENSURE AN EVEN TWIST

THE RIGHT AND THE WRONG
WAY TO TWIST A LOOP

WRONG

RIGHT

Fig. 25. WIRE TRACE MAKING

Now that we have discussed all manner of knots and loops there remains the important matter of lashing a hook to a length of gut substitute. To accomplish this take up the hook in your left hand, and, commencing about one-eighth of an inch from the end of the shank of the hook, wind on about eight turns of binding silk towards the left, then back again over the same eight turns towards the right. Next take your length of gut and, after flattening the end with your teeth, lay it along the shank of the hook. Then wind the silk over both gut and hook shank firmly, until the end of the gut is covered. Wind back again towards the right until the end of the shank is all but reached. At this juncture we want a secure and neat method of finishing off our binding, and it is best achieved by what is known as the "whip finish."

The description which follows should be read in conjunction with Figure 26, as it is an operation which I find very difficult to describe in words. Raise a loop of silk above the hook, as in figure A of the diagram; then complete the loop as in figure B. Now pull the gut through the loop as in figure C, and continue winding two or three turns with the loop of binding silk towards the right. Pull on the free end of binding silk so that the loop ceases to exist, and slip off the spare end short against the shank of the hook. The final action is to finish off the whipping with a dab of varnish or Rawlplug Durofix. We now have an extremely neat and secure fastening, and one which I may say is in use for most kinds of whipping, whether on fishing rods, tackle, polo sticks or cricket bat handles.

With that we will leave the matter of knots and loops and turn our attention to the line proper. The first point which comes to mind is the important matter of splicing a line. I have seen many weird and wonderful joints in a line, ranging from a simple knot (likely to catch in the line guard of the reel and in all the rings of the rod), to a marvellous hard "bobble" resembling a moth's cocoon, which the owner described to me as a "really strong splice, my dear fellah!"

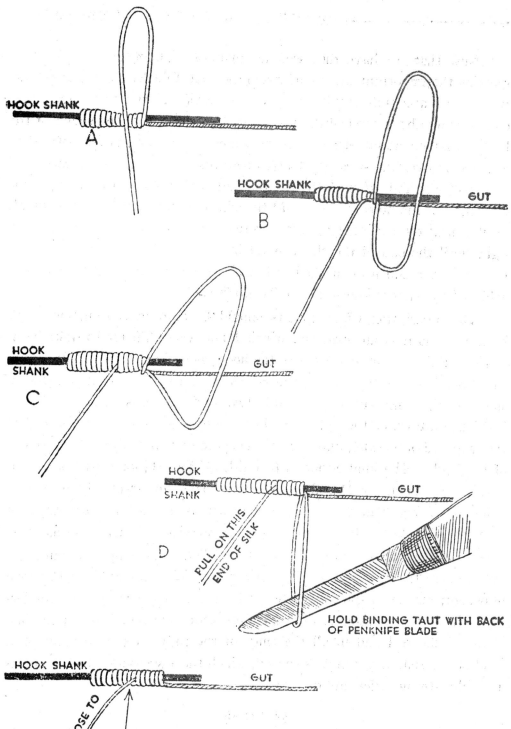

HOOK SHANK

A

HOOK SHANK   GUT

B

HOOK
SHANK   GUT

C

HOOK
SHANK   GUT

D

PULL ON THIS
END OF SILK

HOLD BINDING TAUT WITH BACK
OF PENKNIFE BLADE

HOOK SHANK   GUT

E

CUT OFF CLOSE TO
BINDING

Fig. 26.   THE WHIP FINISH

A good strong neat and serviceable splice is by no means difficult to achieve. The chief requirements are someone to hold the ends of the line, some waxed thread, and some quickdrying varnish. Get your assistant to hold taut a short length of one of the pieces of line to be spliced. Bind it with waxed thread for about a quarter of an inch, and finish off. Now lay the piece of line to be spliced to it alongside, and your assistant holds both pieces taut and alongside one another. Starting about quarter of an inch to the right of the binding already there, bind the two together for a full three-quarters of an inch or more, and then back again, finishing off with a whip finish. The splice will occupy about three-quarters of an inch or so in all, and should now be varnished over with some quick-drying *flexible* varnish. Alternatively it may be waxed over. Personally I prefer to use varnish.

Speaking of varnishes and waxes, here are two recipes for making your own. First, a clear celluloid varnish, the recipe of which is given in Mr. Wanless's book *"The Modern Practical Angler."* I have found it eminently suitable for all manner of fishing needs.

"Celluloid Varnish, made by dissolving small pieces of celluloid in equal quantities of acetone and amyl acetate." *

The next home recipe is one for a good liquid and transparent wax. It is culled from that great book on fly-tying *"How To Tie Flies For Trout,"* by H. G. McClelland. "Melt together in a jam-pot, or other vessel, immersed in boiling water, some of the best and purest white amber resin, with about the same volume of turpentine. Voila tout, the wax is made." †

Earlier in the book I promised a description of how to set about making spinning flights for natural bait. The requirements are some sheet celluloid 1/32 part of an inch in thickness, some stout killin wire, a

---

* *Op. cit. page* 101.　　　　　　　† *Op. cit. page* 53.

pair of scissors, a pair of pliers, treble hooks and gut substitute. First cut out a piece of celluloid into the shape shown in figure 27 opposite. Take a short length of wire and, passing it through the hole in the celluloid "cut," twist it hard up against the celluloid. Lead may be mounted on the wire to the weight required by means of either a small barrel lead or by twisting on a sufficient quantity of lead wire. To seat the lead well it should be given two or three coats of celluloid varnish. Setting aside what we have already done to dry, we take up a swivel, a short length of gut substitute, and a treble hook. To one end we mount the treble hook, by means of one of the knots described earlier, and then attach the mounted hook to the swivel. For both the attachment of the hook and the mounting to the swivel I strongly advocate the method with soft bait mounting wire and the use of an eyed hook.

All that remains now is to attach the mounted hook and swivel to the leaded spinner, and it is easily done with a piece of killin wire. Pass the wire through the hole in the celluloid and the bottom eye of the swivel and twist twice, finishing off with the spare end of wire.

Finally, dip the pliers into some boiling water, and with the heated pliers bend the celluloid vanes to give the necessary spin to the bait. The spinner is now made. You will notice that the pull of the hook from the fish's mouth is directly communicated to the line, and is not attached to the celluloid of the spinner. This type of spinner may be made in whatever size you require, whether for threadline use or for heavier gear. The treble hook should lie just below the anal fin of the bait. I prefer only one treble hook, as it obviates the case of a pricked fish when they come short. (See also Fig. No. 6).

But what of the baits themselves? It is not always possible to get a supply of fresh bait at the water-side. I always use preserved baits, as

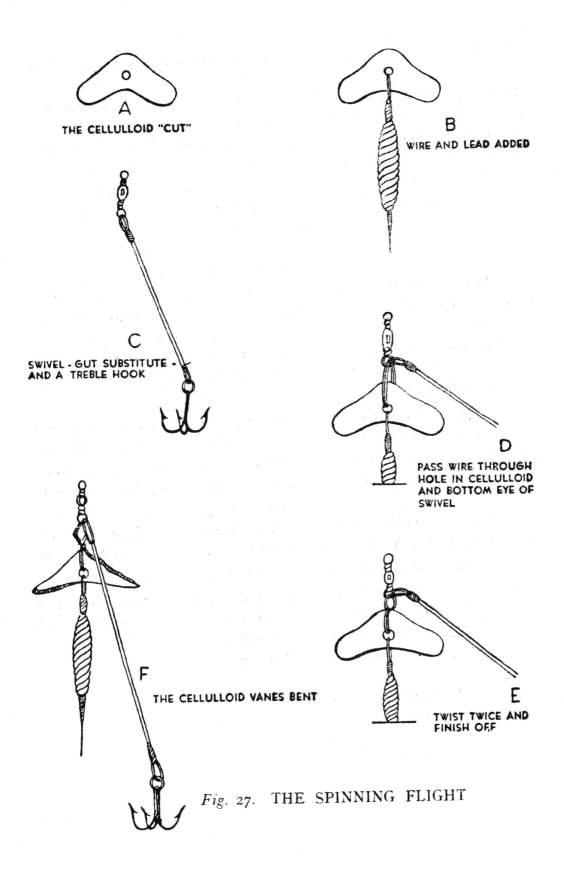

THE CELLULLOID "CUT"

A

B

WIRE AND LEAD ADDED

C

SWIVEL - GUT SUBSTITUTE -
AND A TREBLE HOOK

D

PASS WIRE THROUGH
HOLE IN CELLULLOID
AND BOTTOM EYE OF
SWIVEL

F

THE CELLULLOID VANES BENT

E

TWIST TWICE AND
FINISH OFF

Fig. 27. THE SPINNING FLIGHT

they are tougher and always handy. Any local netsman will provide hundreds of natural small fish for a few annas. To preserve Chilwa or Stone Loach, put them in a solution of one part formalin to twenty parts of water. Leave the baits in this solution for a fortnight, then take them out and wash them and trim off the fins. Replace them in the following solution in a screw-topped jam-jar, in which they will keep indefinitely :—

> Formalin ½ ounce,
> Glycerine 1 ounce,
> Distilled Water 5 ounces.

If a golden-red colour is desired for the baits, add a little red ink. This golden-red colour frequently has a most tonic effect on non-taking fish. When bottling natural bait, ensure that the vessel in which they are to be placed is large enough for the baits to lie straight. Pickling toughens the minnows, and there is nothing so infuriating as trying to mount a bait which has a kink in it, (*crede experto !*)

To make a plug : take a well-seasoned piece of wood (the ideal is a piece of the head of an old polo stick) and fashion it by means of sandpaper, knife and saw into the cigar-like shape shewn in figure 28 opposite. So far so good. Now take a round piece of wool about half an inch in diameter and around it wrap some coarse sandpaper. With it file away on the line A—A until a groove is worn of about three-eighths of an inch in depth to the line A—B. A—B should be at an angle of approximately 45° to the main axis of the plug, and proceed as in diagram.

Next item, "colouring the brute." This is a matter for the angler to decide in the light of experience on his chosen river. Personally, I find that the following combinations of colour kill in most waters :—

    (a) Olive green back with yellow strip down the centre and white belly.

    (b) Blue back and white belly.

    (c) Brown back with red spots and white belly.

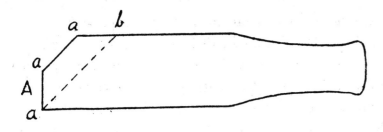

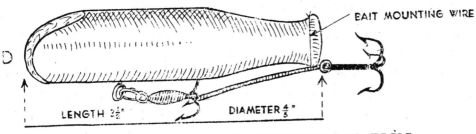

BAIT MOUNTING WIRE

LENGTH 3½"   DIAMETER ⅘"

Fig. 28. GENERAL PURPOSE 3½" PLUG

A. Roughly Shaped wood.,
B. The groove in place.
C. Sharp corners rounded off for better streamline and the tail formed.
D. The finished plug with hooks added. Note how the tail hook is attacked to the body of the plug with a strand of bait mounting wire or thread.

Finally, to add the hooks and attachment for fastening the trace, use small screw eyes. By small I mean small in the eye but long in the shank. The actual eye should be closed and soldered to prevent it opening when into a powerful fish. Fix one in the centre of the groove and a third of the way from the top, and another on the belly of the plug as shewn in the diagram. Two No. 5 size trebles should be whipped to a short length of cable wire and attached by means of a Hardy Link to the bottom screw eye – *Voici c'est complet* !

When fishing the hooks should be bound to the body of the plug by means of a turn of soft bait binding wire, which will break when a fish strikes, thus leaving only the hooks in his mouth.

This plug may be made either large or small for use with either the threadline or with the multiplier. For especial use with the threadline there is a little jointed model which I have found satisfactory. Figure 29 shows it in various stages of construction. When making plugs for threadline use, it is essential to add a small lead insert into the belly of the bait in order to keel them. Furthermore, ensure that the swivels on the trace are working freely, as otherwise these little plugs have a nasty habit of turning over in the water.

Make the heads of all small plugs large enough ; their stability in swimming depends on the streamline effect in the water, and if the taper is not well marked from the head to the tail streamlining is lost.

Since we have been playing with sandpaper and paint, let us now turn our hands to making a float. We shall require some porcupine quills of various lengths and some medicine-bottle corks. Taking up four corks we punch a hole through the centre of each and impale them on a five-inch quill, as in X of figure 30. With sandpaper and a knife we fashion them so that the float takes shape as in Y of the figure. Picking up the paint brushes we will colour our float white for two-thirds of the way and then red for one third, with white again for the quill standing out of the

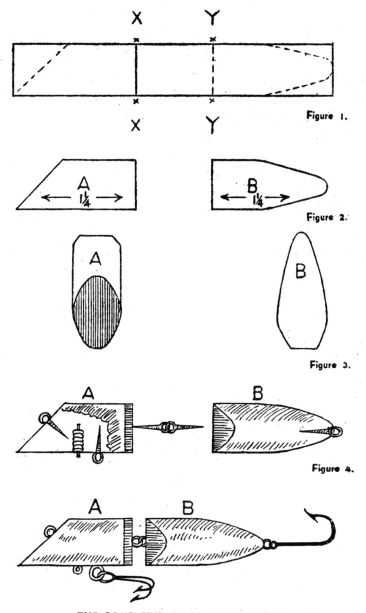

Figure 1.

Figure 2.

Figure 3.

Figure 4.

THE COMPLETED PLUG (TOTAL LENGTH 2¾″)

Directions.—Shape a round piece of wood of ½ inch diameter with knife and sandpaper as shewn by the dotted lines in figure 1. Saw through at x–x and y–y, and the two pieces A and B result. With knife and sandpaper further shape them as in figure 3. A lead insert is now fixed in piece A by means of lead wire, a small screw and Rawlplug Durofix. Screw eyes are inserted as shewn and hooks attached. The pieces A and B are then jointed by means of linked screw eyes and the plug is complete except for colouring.

Fig. 29. THREADLINE PLUG

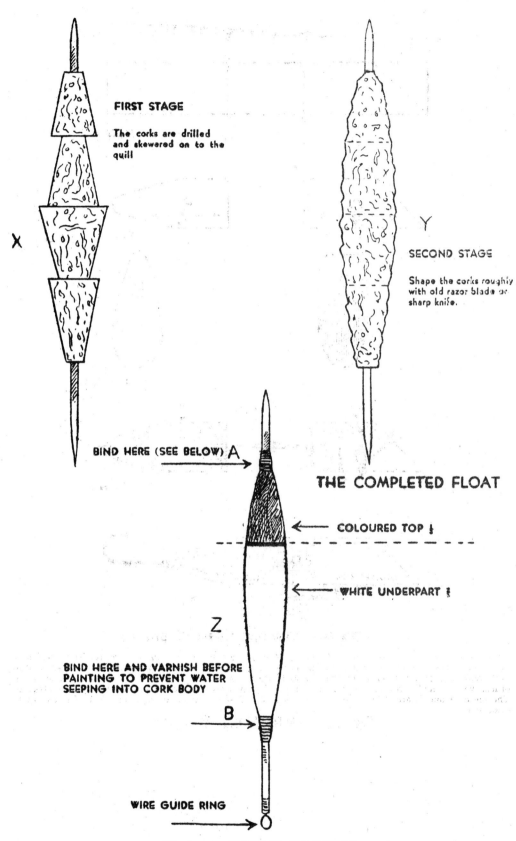

FIRST STAGE

The corks are drilled and skewered on to the quill

X

SECOND STAGE

Shape the corks roughly with old razor blade or sharp knife.

Y

THE COMPLETED FLOAT

BIND HERE (SEE BELOW) A

COLOURED TOP ½

WHITE UNDERPART ½

Z

BIND HERE AND VARNISH BEFORE PAINTING TO PREVENT WATER SEEPING INTO CORK BODY

B

WIRE GUIDE RING

Fig. 30. FLOAT MAKING

cork at the top. Before painting we bind and varnish the junctions of cork and quill at A and B, and whip on a small wire ring to the bottom of the quill for the line. For attachment of the line at the top end use a small rubber band. The rubber rings sold by stationers in the finer sizes will do ; if they are too big cut them in half and knot the ends. They are used doubled, trebled or quadrupled, and are a lot superior to the old-fashioned quill-cap which is always splitting. Furthermore, the attachment of a feather as described in Chapter VI is much easier with a rubber ring.

Finally we shall tie a few lures for use with the threadline. Fly-dressing is a simple process, so divorce from your mind any idea of difficulty or knack. The following impedimenta are required :—

(a) An assortment of hooks – really fine wire ones – sizes 10 to 14.

(b) Some fly-tying silk (a great variety of colours are not necessary ; orange and purple will do.)

(c) Liquid wax and celluloid varnish, as described earlier.

(d) Fly-dressers' tweezers.

(e) A sharp pair of pointed scissors.

(f) Feathers – tinsel – coloured wool (stolen from your wife) – a large darning needle – and some fine lead wire.

Sit down in a good light and spread the above items out on a white background – a large sheet of blotting paper is excellent. Let us start by dressing a 3-hook Coachman lure. First whip the hooks to a two-inch length of gut – the top hook should be eyed of course. Next wind on to the hook shanks and intervening gut some fine lead wire. Bind the beginning and the end of the lead wire with tying silk and leave the shank of the top hook clear for one-third to a quarter of an inch, depending on the size of hook you are using.

FIRST WHIP THE HOOKS TO GUT

NEXT WIND ON SOME FINE LEAD WIRE

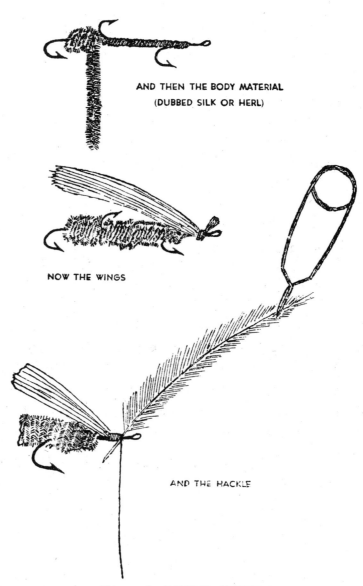

AND THEN THE BODY MATERIAL
(DUBBED SILK OR HERL)

NOW THE WINGS

AND THE HACKLE

Fig 31. LURE TYING

Next take a peacock "herl" and bind one end securely to the bottom hook just below where the lead wire ends. Herls are woolly strips of plume taken from the large feathers of the peacock. The ones we shall need are those from the lower part of the tail which are a fine red bronze in colour, or those from the sword feathers, which are a hard metallic green. We shall use the red bronze herl for the fly we are now tying.

Next cut off the spare end of silk and wind the peacock herl over the lead wire so that it is entirely covered. A single herl will not be long enough to make the body of the fly, so when it comes to an end tie in another herl and continue. The operation of tying in the end of one herl and the start of the next may be done with one binding of silk. When the lead wire is completely covered, fasten the herl with a few turns of tying silk and clip off the spare end.

Now select a white wing or tail feather from which to prepare the wings. Cut away a piece of feather web half an inch broad. Take the severed piece of feather web in both hands and very gently rub it between finger and thumb until it assumes a rectangular shape. The wings are now ready to tie in. Double the feather web in half and, taking it by the roots with the finger and thumb of the right hand, lay it on the upper side of the exposed shank of the top hook. Then place the tips of the finger and thumb of the left hand on either side of the hook and hold the wings in position, and bind on with tying silk, finishing off with a half hitch and leaving the end of the silk free.

Next take up a hackle feather of dark russet brown and prepare it by stripping off the down from the lower end of the hackle stem or quill. Then, holding by the tip, lay the root end of the quill obliquely across the under side of the hook shank, and using the free end of silk mentioned above, tie in with two or three turns, and finish with a half hitch. Again leave the spare end of tying silk free. Cut away the exposed end of the hackle stem. Grip the point of the hackle feather with the spring fly-tying tweezers and hold the spare end of tying silk taut with the right hand. Now wind the hackle two or three turns to the right. Bring the turns alternately behind and in front of the taut length of tying silk, always pulling the point of the hackle slightly to the right when passing underneath the shank of the hook. Then, holding the unwound end of the hackle taut and pointing to the right, fasten down the wound part with tying silk, winding towards the right, and finish with a half hitch. Cut away the spare end of the hackle and make a whip finish with the end of the tying silk. Cut off the spare end of silk and give the whip finish a dab of varnish with the point of the darning needle. The lure is now complete.

In case anyone should not know what a hackle is, may I explain that it is the short pointed feather taken from the back of the neck of a bird. They may be bought dyed in any colour from a good tackleist or be used in their natural colours as plucked from the bird.

The "bodies" of lures may be of various materials, such as flat silver tinsel (which may be bought on little wooden reels), or of what is known technically to fly-dressers as dubbing. In the case of tinsel bodies, they are tied in the same manner as the peacock herl body described above. Dubbed bodies are a little more difficult. When the lead wire has been wound on the fly, tie in a piece of waxed silk at the lower end. Now take up a small quantity of wool or fur and tease it out well, and, taking a little up between the finger and thumb, rub it gently round the waxed thread so that it adheres. When two or three inches of thread have been so covered, use it to make the body of the fly.

I append here the dressings of some well-known and well-tried lures for Himalayan trout.

The Dandy Lure. Silver tinsel body, fox-red hackle and wings of barred teal feather.

The Jungle Lure. Silver body, black hackle and "wings" of four or five peacock herls from the sword feathers with a small jungle cock "eye" feather on each side. Alternatively, the hackle may be the speckled feather of a black partridge, and a red tab of wool tied in at the tail.

Teal and Green.   Body green wool dubbed on to tying silk, and with a silver tinsel tip.   Hackle light olive green or natural grey partridge hackle.   "Wings" barred teal feather.

March Brown.   Body, wool cut from a hare's ear and dubbed on to waxed silk.   Hackle natural grey partridge.   "Wings" cut from the tail feather of a female pheasant, or from the brown wing feather of a mallard duck.   Two or three long fibres of the wing material should be tied in at the tail to form whisks.

Alexandra.   Silver tinsel body, "wings" peacock herl of bright metallic green with a few fibres of pink flamingo feather added. Hackle of black or dark olive green.

Butcher.   Silver tinsel body, black hackle and "wings" cut from the black wing feather of the crow.

Of the above selection the March Brown should be tied either on a largish single hook (say size 5) or with two small hooks tied close together. The same applies to the Alexandra and the Butcher when they are to represent insects, but they may also be tied large and used as spinning lures too. (See Chapter V.)

One last lure remains : that is my own Bi-Colour Frog Lure.   The armament for this fly should be a size 6 eyed single hook and a small size 14 treble tied together as in Fig. 14, page 74. Lead should be tied from the junction of the gut with the single hook to the head of the little treble. Thus the lure when in action will always sink by the tail.   Two streamers of brown kid leather should now be tied in.   Then, starting at the head of the little tail treble, a large natural partridge hackle should be tied in, followed by a large white hackle, and then another partridge hackle. These hackle feathers must be bushy as they form the body as well as the hackle of the fly.   The finished product should then appear as shown in the diagram.

THE list of fishes that follows is limited to those likely to be encountered by the fisherman using light tackle, either in the hill streams of the Punjab or where those streams merge from the hills and enter the plains. I do not pretend that it is in any way complete, being compiled from notes in my own fishing diary and from information from my fishing friends and acquaintances.

As I am nothing of a scientist, and observe the fishes I catch purely from interest, I have omitted scientific terminology as much as possible. For those who wish to enquire more deeply, I recommend a study of *The Angler in India*, and of Col. Masters' book *The Complete Indian Angler.* In the latter publication there are delightful pencil drawings of most of the Indian fishes. The naturalist who has this book by him will have no difficulty in distinguishing and naming correctly any fish which he may be fortunate enough to land.

The fins of fishes are divided into two groups – paired fins and vertical fins. The pairs of fins consist of the *Pectorals*, which are situated in the fore-part of the body and correspond to the forelegs of an animal, and the *Ventrals*, which are situated on the lower surface of the after-part of the fish and correspond to the hind legs of an animal. Neither of these pairs of fins are used in swimming, and either or both of these pairs may be absent in any species of fish. Of the vertical fins there is the *Dorsal* which is on the middle line of the back ; this may be either in one piece or divided. The Anal fin is situated on the longitudinal line of the belly. Finally there is the *Caudal* fin which forms part of the tail of a fish, and is its main power for propulsion through the water and is comparable to the propeller of a ship.

As most fishes continue to grow as long as they live, the actual length of a fish is useless as a criterion of judgement of its value as a capture. The essential point is the relative measurements of various parts of its body to its length when determining weight by calculation. It is certainly a better method of finding the weight of a fish by calculation than to rely on the very doubtful results shewn by the lying scales or balances which will be produced, shall we say, by the Dak Bungalow Khansamah. There are various formulae for estimating the weight of a fish by calculation. In the Journal of the Bombay Natural History Society,* Major W. B. Trevenen gives us the following formula, which is, I think, the safest to use for accurate results with all types of Indian fishes. The tendency is perhaps to slightly under-estimate, but the error is almost negligible.

$$\frac{(L \frac{1}{4}L) \times (G)^2}{1000} = \text{Weight}$$

G = The greatest girth of the fish.

L = The length of the fish taken from the closed
      mouth to the fork in the tail.

The Mahseer. Though my friend Barbus Tor (the mahseer) has been discussed in some detail already I feel that a few more notes regarding him will not come amiss, as he is the *piece de resistance* in our gallery. It is an extraordinary thing how mahseer are never seen in the act of spawning. If this occurred when the rivers were low and clear it would not be difficult to observe them. The only occasions on which I have taken ripe fish, full of milt, is at the beginning of the rains or just before. I feel that it may be safely assumed, therefore, that the end of June to the beginning of September is the period when this fish is best left alone to propagate his species. After the rains, except for a few fish which will remain in the deep pools of the small streams, the mahseer all tend to

---

*Op. Cit. Vol. XXX. p. 711.

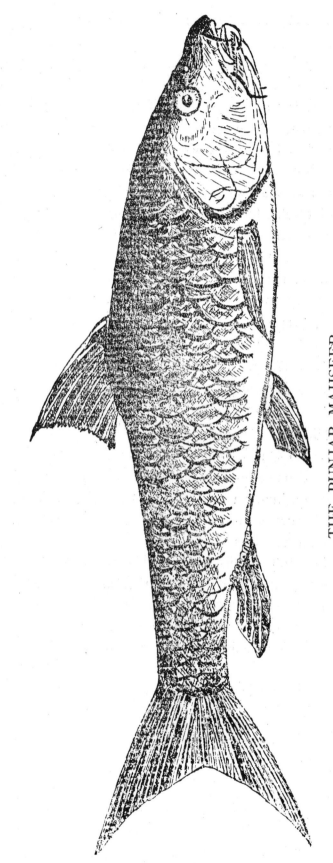

THE PUNJAB MAHSEER
From Life
(Beas River)

collect in the deepest pools in the foothills where the mountain streams debouch on to the plains and join the big rivers. During December, January and early February, when the weather is cold, the fish will be found gathered together in deep water for warmth.

I have observed three distinct forms of colouring on the mahseer I have taken in the Punjab. The most common is a silvery fish, dark olive green on the back, and with a golden tinge on the scales along the lateral line. The fins are golden red. He is a very handsome game looking fish. The second colouring that I have observed in the Punjab is an almost red mahseer. These are very rare and I have only seen them in the Chenab River at Marala and in the Jammu Tawi above Jammu town. Perhaps those I have observed were cases of albinism. The third type is a very dark fish with an almost black back. This is, however, not the black mahseer of further south, I am sure, as it has the golden orange fins of the true Punjab mahseer.

Locality and diet have a marked effect on the colouring of fish. My friend, Mr. A. M. David, whose knowledge of Indian fishes and fishing is encyclopaedic, writes me as follows :– "Regarding your query of locality and colour variation : this is particularly marked in the Kulu Trout. Some fish I took from the Tirthan River looked suspiciously like Brown-Rainbow Hybrids, but a closer examination and reports from experts in England showed them to be Brown Trout with a local colour variation." I feel that I am correct in the assumption, therefore, that there is but one Mahseer of the Punjab, and that variations of colour, and in some instances even of shape, are due entirely to the effect of local conditions.

Though in Chapter IV I have spoken of the best weather conditions for successful fishing, there are one or two points which I feel would be of interest to fishermen which I will mention here. The first is the question of the full moon. Personally I have never been able to do any good with manseer at the period of full moon. The fish at this time become very sullen and will not take a spinning bait. I have caught them with bait, however, in backwaters and deep pools. The full moon is a time to be avoided if you are planning a fishing trip. There was a keen fisherman who worked out this matter of lunar influence very carefully, and by putting his theory into practice he took many hundreds of pounds of fish out of the Beas River. He started with the angle of incidence of the moon on the waters, and almost proved that a very acute angle gave marvellous results— water and weather being favourable.

Mahseer do not normally come on the take well till the sun is on the water, though too much of it puts them down. Many anglers of my acquaintance get up at the screech of dawn, or even before, to start their fishing day. But my experience leads me to believe that until the sun is well on the water the fishing is not worth the early rising entailed. This is, however, a very controversial matter, as I know of forty-pounders taken at dawn. My views are based on my own fishing experiences. Another theory beloved of many is that the early-rising angler gets into the big fish when they are moving out of the shallows, they have been feeding all night, to lie up during the day in the deep shady pools. Another time when the fishing is not at its best is the middle of the day. The angler is much better advised to take the opportunity of a good rest between the hours of twelve-thirty and two, particularly if there is much water to be covered ; he will fish much better for not being over-tired. As Noel Coward has wittily said in his famous *Mad Dogs and Englishmen* :—

> Mad dogs and Englishmen
> Go out in the midday sun
> In the mangrove swamps
> Where the python romps
> There is peace from twelve till two.
> Even cariboos lie down and snooze

For there's nothing else to do.

. . . .

In a jungle town where the sun beats down
To the rage of man and beast,
The English garb of the English Sahib
Merely gets a bit more creased."

Well, I don't suggest that mangrove swamps are the best place for fishing, but nevertheless there is a lot in what he says. You have been warned.

Excluding periods of full moon, which are uniformly bad, if you can plan your fishing to coincide with the times when high tide would occur, were the water of your choice a part of the sea, success is assured. This may sound somewhat far-fetched, but carefully recorded observations over the last two years have proved to me, at any rate, the truth of this statement, not only with mahseer but with all kinds of fish. If high tide should coincide with the usual time of the morning or the evening take you will unquestionably have a great time. There is a lot to be said scientifically for this theory. Fish are more affected by the pressure of the water than anything else that lives therein. In the sea, high tide brings food to the fish, and the pressure of the water on their bodies is less, hence they are more alive and therefore hungrier. There is no reason to believe that the same does not occur in fresh water. Here the bulk of the water is smaller and therefore a rise or an increase in its volume is not noticeable, but the lessening of pressure is definitely present.

Many with whom I have discussed my "tidal" theory claim that my argnment is fallacious on the grounds that the rise and fall in rivers fed by glaciers (and this is true of most Punjab rivers) is governed by the fact that the bulk of the water varies with the freezing and thawing of the glaciers. Others argue that the influence of the Punjab canal systems is alone sufficient to upset the "Tidal Theory." But, though ready to admit

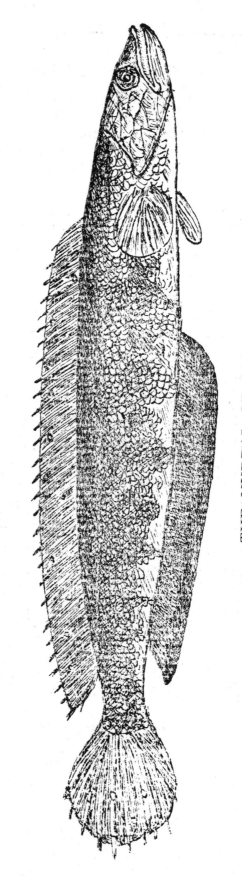

THE MURRAL OR SAUL

From Life

(Jammu Tawi River)

that the visible bulk of the water is governed by these natural facts, I am still of the opinion that the physical phenomena which causes tides must have an effect of increase or decrease in the water pressure and its oxygen content, and hence on the fish themselves. As tides are affected by the moon, I submit that it is logical to assume that the moon must be the cause of good or bad fishing. I should be happy to correspond with any fisherman who is willing to make observations and to record his results with this very interesting theory, if only to prove it a *post hoc ergo propter hoc* fallacy !

The worst possible days for mahseer fishing are those when the sky is overcast with cloud and direct rays of the sun do not touch the water. I consider that there is a special form of glare which affects the fish under such conditions, and they are not able to see the bait properly on account of it.

Before closing my notes on "Barbus Tor," I draw attention to the very pleasant trophy which is provided by his gill teeth. These are situated well down in the throat below the gills. If suitably cleaned and mounted on a little shield of *shisham* wood, they make a very pleasant memento of a happy day's sport.

Well, so much for my friend the Mahseer, a very handsome fellow and a gallant gentleman. Long may be flourish !

The next on my list of fishes is **the Mural.** (Also called Saul in the Punjab). The murral in his feeding is very like the pike of European waters. He does not like rocky or shingly bottom, but is usually found in pools where the water moves slowly over a bed of mud and in still water The murral is very good eating – probably one of the best fresh-water fish in India for the table. Sometimes he is a little muddy, but this can be overcome by soaking him in a brine solution for two or three hours. Unlike most Indian fishes, the murral has a single skeleton, and one therefore does not stand in dread of sudden death from a bone in the throat· when he appears on the table.

The best bait I know for this fish is a highly-coloured plug. The more colour the better, particularly when red is to the fore. This should be worked near the surface of the water, as murral are very fond of basking near the surface in the sun. When you hook a murral the important thing to do is to keep as hard a strain on him as you dare, as they have a very bony mouth in which hooks do not take a good hold. As long as the strain is there the fish will hang on like grim death, but if the strain is relaxed for a minute the murral will, if possible, eject the bait. Murral are found in great numbers in tanks, and in stretches of water which are flooded every now and again from a nearby stream. They love reedy banks where they lie in wait for unsuspecting frogs and small fry. They will take almost any form of life that moves. I have seen them take mice and fledglings that have dropped into the water.

The Murral is perhaps the most interesting fish that exists in India. Its home is in a hole in a mud bank, and should the tank or backwater dry up the murral buries itself in the mud and remains there till the rains come again and cover his lie with water. It is said that murral run to quite considerable weight. Personally I have never caught one in a stream or river over ten pounds, and neither have I met anyone else who has done so, though I believe that they attain two or three times this weight. Murral are able to travel short distances over land ; this they do in search of new waters when their own home becomes dry. In appearance the Murral is a handsome fish, and is easily recognised. It has a snake-like head with scale-like markings thereon. The dorsal fin runs from just behind the head the whole length of the body to the tail, to which it is not joined. The anal fin starts about one-third of the way down the body and runs to the tail, which it does not join. Both the dorsal and anal fins are spineless. There are quite a few varieties of murral to be had ; the two most usually caught are coloured as follows :

The first is a very dark olive green on the back, with light and dark bands on the side. The rays of the fins also project beyond the webbing. This is called the banded mural. (*vide* illustration.)

The second type is not so heavily built and is marked with square and triangular spots along the central line of the body. It also has a distinctive white ringed spot on the caudal fin.

The habits of both are the same. When you hook a mural, as likely as not he will run straight towards you, taking a sudden right-angle turn when he catches sight of you. Sometimes they play very well, leaping out of the water frequently and in the most spectacular manner, and worrying the bait like a dog. Alternatively he may plunge straight down into the weeds if any are about, from which he is the very devil to get out.

Murral are always on the watch-out for anything coming into the water off the bank, so if conditions permit cast your bait on to the bank and from there flop it into the water.

They are reported to show a certain amount of parental affection for their young, and are, I believe—together with the stickleback of home waters—unique in this respect.

The Mulley, (also called Wallago attu). Mulley are revolting-looking fish. They have an enormous head with a cavernous mouth full of very sharp teeth, and when you catch one of them be careful when handling, as they can give a very nasty bite. Directly below and behind the head is an obscene paunch, round like a bladder. The remainder of the body is flat-sided, with the anal fin running practically the whole length of the body but just stopping short of the pelvic and caudal fins, to which it is not joined. The mulley has two long feelers on the top of his snout; these, I think, he uses as an extra pair of eyes when the water is coloured. He has also two barbels underneath his mouth. In colouring the mulley is a silvery fish with a metallic green tinge on the back. They are scaleless, and have a well-marked lateral line from the gill plates to the tail.

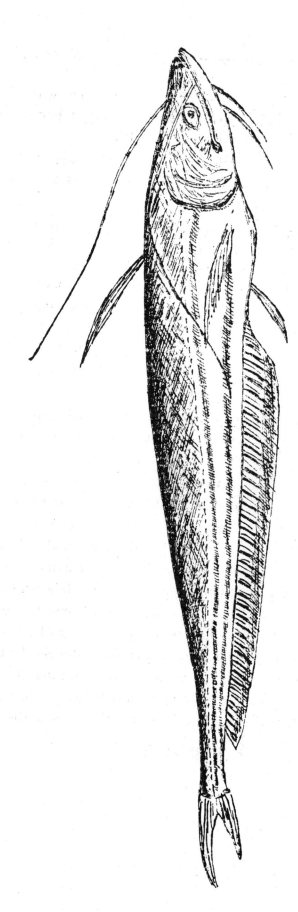

MULLEY (WALLAGO ATTU)
Also called the Freshwater Shark
From life
(Chenab River)

These fish are remarkable in that they often hunt in pairs. When the chilwa are running and the water is clear, it is often possible to see a pair of mulleys herding the wretched little fish together as though on a pre-arranged plan, and darting in and grabbing as many as they can, only to fall back in a few moments into their original position in order to repeat the operation. It is really a most remarkable sight, and one which is well worth watching ; the movement of the mulley is so well timed, and the herding together of the chilwa so well carried out, that an observer is forced to the conclusion that the mulley have decided on the plan of action beforehand.

Mulley belongs to the family of Siluridae, which embraces all fish which are familiarly termed fresh-water sharks. They are scavengers and do a lot of good in cleaning up the river bed. As such they take most kinds of bait on all kinds of tackle. I find that the plug does as well as any, particularly when fished in the evening or early morning. Mulley are then usually near the surface, and often roll half out of the water. They can often be seen with the huge mouth out of water and open like a shrimping net. They will also take natural bait, which is best used at other times of the day, when the mulley are not obviously near the surface ; it should be spun slowly with a sink and draw movement.

Mulley are quite good sporting fish and I have found them to play quite well. If you are too hard on them they will come to the surface and thrash the water in the most frightening manner. When they do this ease the strain, as unless you do, it nearly always ends in a lost fish. When a mulley is played out he becomes a dead weight on the line, owing to his habit of lying back on the current with his cavernous mouth open ; the resultant effect is that of trying to pull an animated bucket against the stream. Wire traces are the only possible thing that will stand up to the rows of teeth in the mulley's mouth.

❧ 129 ❧

THE GOONCH
From Life
(Haro River)

They are good table fish and are seldom muddy in taste. Mulley are reported to grow very large and to attain a length of as much as six feet. I have not caught one over fifteen pounds myself, but know of a monster taken at Marala Weir which weighed some forty pounds. It is said that they may be had as large as one hundred pounds in weight, but I have no information of any such fish ever having been taken on rod and line. Mulley run up hill streams to quite a fair altitude ; the highest I have known them caught is about three thousand five hundred feet.

The Goonch. Like the mulley, a fresh-water shark which grows to a length of six feet. The body is usually a dirty grey with large irregular black or dark brown markings. The fins usually have a dark band across them and have a dark base. The goonch is not a good sporting fish, as, though they take the plug and natural bait readily enough if spun very slowly, they go straight to the bottom, and a pull devil pull baker act ensues, usually ending in favour of the fish. They lie in the extremes of white water and in the depths of the largest pools if there is a current through them. Though a very strong fish they are sullen to a degree and sluggish in their movements on being hooked. Goonch are essentially river fish and are often to be had near the head-works of a canal. I understand that they are often taken at the Okhla Junction near Delhi.

The Butchwa. A very pretty fish with a metallic green back, silver sides and belly, and a markedly forked tail. They grow to some four or five pounds in weight, though usually taken smaller. They are extremely good eating. They play wildly, frequently jumping out of the water, and giving the impression that they are much larger than they really are. Altogether a very sporting little fish. There are many species of catfihes, all of which are scaleless and come under the generic title of Butchwa.

They may be had as far up the Beas as Dehra Gopipur; where they may be taken on spinning tackle above the bridge of boats. Butchwa take a

THE BUTCHWA

From a Photograph

(A generic name for most of the catfishes)

spinning bait readily, and are best fished for with threadline tackle and natural bait mounted in a scarab (see Chapter III). Though the butchwa does not run up to any altitude sufficient to be classed as an inhabitant of mountain streams, they are to be had in any of the Punjab rivers at certain times of the year, where their course lies in the plains. The Sutlej and the Ravi are particularly noted for them.

The Chirroo. The chirroo is a barbel ; he is thick at the shoulder and tapers quickly towards the tail. Like the barbel of European waters he is covered in a thick slime. In colour he is a dark nondescript grey on his back with a number of dark spots. The mouth of the chirroo is placed well underneath and puts one in mind of that of the shark. Though they run up to about fifteen or twenty pounds they are seldom caught so large by fair means. They are not very sporting fish ; when hooked they give you one run and then sulk for a bit, after which they may be reeled in. To get the best from them fish with the threadline. They are to be had in abundance in Kashmir, and take all sorts of baits, the best being worm. They may, however, be taken on spinning tackle, the baby threadline minnows being excellent.

The Choosh. This is another barbel, almost identical in appearance with the chirroo, except that the spots are absent, and he has a yellowish tinge on his underparts. Like the chirroo they run large, but are not often taken over five or six pounds in weight.

Both chirroo and choosh are passable table fish. If caught in large waters they are very apt to be muddy. This muddiness can be cured to a certain extent by soaking them in brine. When taken in a rocky stream they are not too bad, but at no time would I describe them as really palatable.

The Himalayan Mountain Barbel. A true barbel in every way. Though usually described as bottom feeders I have taken these fish on

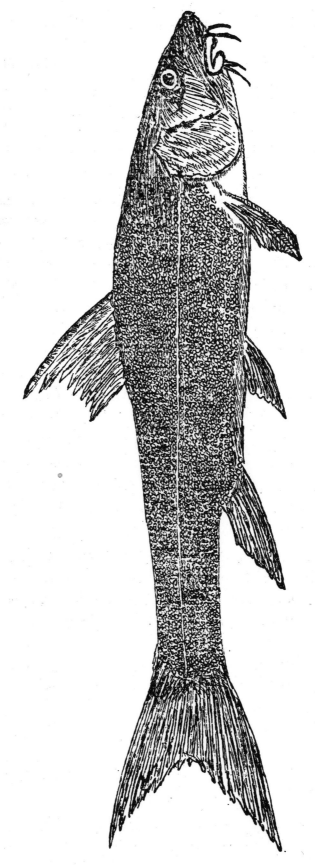

THE CHOOSH

The Chirroo and the Mountain Barbel also resemble this fish closely in shape.

From Life

(Jhelum River)

a spinning bait in Kulu. These fish vary very much in appearance and range from a dirty browny-grey to the pretty fish which, though a dingy brown on the back, has its sides mottled and spotted rather like a trout. They are, in my opinion, revolting from an edible point of view, the flesh on cooking turning out a most unappetising grey colour.

They are often taken in Kulu when fishing in trout waters, and give the wretched fisherman a terrific thrill on first being hooked, as he believes he has got in to the father and mother of a trout. They have a distinctive way of wagging a great trout-like tail on the surface when they are being played. On the whole I should describe them as a sporting fish, particularly if fished for on light threadline tackle, although their habit of getting under a stone leaves much to be desired. Probably this fish, along with the choosh and chirroo, would rank higher in the hierarchy of sporting fishes if they did not inhabit waters in which trout have now been acclimatised. Nevertheless they are well worth fishing for, particularly if the threadline is used.

Trout. Last but by no means least in my list of fishes is the trout. Though not indigenous to Indian waters they are now so well-established in the waters to which they have been introduced in this country that I feel that they may almost be described as Indian fishes. Trout in India are of two kinds, the Brown Trout (*salmo fario*) and the Rainbow Trout (*salmo irideus*). Of the two the brown trout has taken most kindly to such streams in which it has been planted. The rainbow is a doubtful quantity, owing to its habit of entirely disappearing from waters in which it has been placed. A successful crossing of rainbow and brown trout was carried out in Kulu, but the results of the experiment did not justify its further continuance.

A description of the trout would be redundant in this book, but a word or two on how to distinguish the rainbow from the brown trout would not, I think, come amiss. The chief point which is noticeable is that the rainbow has a more generous distribution of smaller speckling on its fins and body than the brownie. The Brown trout has the beautiful red spots on its flanks, which are absent with the Rainbow. It has also very beautiful spectroscopically-coloured bands and blotches on its body giving it the name of Rainbow Trout.

The food of both rainbow and brown trout consists mainly of worms, frogs, small fish, fresh-water shrimps, and the under-water larvae of flies, and beetles of all kinds. It is my firm belief that, with the abundance of underwater food that obtains in Indian streams, the trout do not feed on the surface fly to a sufficient degree to warrant the fisherman using it as a form of bait to any serious extent. That they rise to the fly and that they may be taken on the artificial fly (as distinct from the lure) is a fact not to be denied, but for serious fishing the fly is best left alone if good sport is looked for.

MASHEER RIVER

Plate XI   A NICE MULLEY

Chapter IX LOCALITIES AND THE FISHING REGISTER

*L*OCALITY knowledge is three-quarters of the success of any fishing trip. Normally it is only picked up as the result of years of observation and practice, and after much enquiry from older hands at the game. Luckily, fishermen in India have the great advantage of being able to refer to Skene Dhu's *Angler in Northern India*, which gives very full details of most of the fishable streams north of the Nerbudda. Though written some years ago this book is still very much up-to-date, and is a mine of information which few keen anglers can afford to be without.

The catalogue of localities which follows in the next few pages in no way pretends to be a complete Gazetteer of Punjab Fishings. It does, however, describe waters which are entirely suitable for the light fisher, and will, I hope, give sufficient information to the newcomer and beginner to enable him to start with his fishing without further ado. I have divided my list of localities into areas covered by the main districts of the Punjab, with a final section devoted entirely to trout fishing, irrespective of geographical position.

Rawalpindi District. The best recommendation for fishing in this area is a trip by boat from Attock to Khushalgarh. Hire a large country boat and take complete camping kit so that two or three days may be spent on the trip. All manner of fish are to be had in this stretch of the Indus, and if carrying out the expedition with the aid of a boat one can fish the many fine pools and runs with ease and leisure. The trip is best attempted in March when the chilwa are running. The most successful baits are without doubt the Heddon River Runt Spook Shore Minnows (silver and gold). In really deep stretches the large spoon may be used. Natural bait is, surprisingly enough, remarkable in its lack of success. Prawn is entirely excellent.

There are a number of smaller rivers around Pindi such as the Rawal, the Sohan, the Chiblat, and the Haro. Most of them are so overworked that no great hopes of large fish may be entertained. It is worth while going to Hasan Abdal along the Peshawar road ; drive through the village to the bridge over the river about a mile beyond. The pool below the bridge has yielded quite a fair number of decent fish, particularly when the water has just cleared after the monsoon. Then fish down to the junction of the Haro and the Chiblat ; this is a good stretch and contains some very fair fish. From the junction of the two streams right down to the main junction with the Indus is all good water. There are quite a few murral in the stream near Pigeon Cliffs.

Wilsons the Chemists in Rawalpindi are stockists of fishing tackle, and will always give information regarding licences and permits. They will also inform one of the fishing conditions.

Popcorn fishing is much practised in this district, and using the method described in Chapter VI, I have on occasions had quite reasonable sport. In May the mulberry fished in the same way is also worth while. Threadline tackle is by far the best in the small streams.

There is some quite good mahseer fishing to be had at Domel and Kohala in the Jhelum River, but only when the water is clear. Both places are reached *via* the Srinagar Road.

Jhelum District. Tangrot is remarkable in that, from September to the middle of June the visiting angler may always hope to catch fish. It is the junction of the Poonch and the Jhelum Rivers. There is a very fine long pool (Jungoo Pool) at the junction which is fished from a boat. A word of warning here. Do not let yourself be persuaded to troll by the local shikari. With the short rod it is possible to cast a long line, so make the most of it. Trolling is ruinous to lines, and if you do troll a great deal of lost tackle will be your reward. It is a stupid, lazy form of fishing anyway ; use the boat by all means : it is very nearly impossible to fish the place at all without one ; but cast —— don't troll.

Fish here run very large, hence the larger form of plug is to be recommended. A large jointed Pal-O'-Mine will do execution under most conditions. If the water is dirty use a silver or light-coloured plug. The majority of good fish at Tangrot have been taken on a large spoon. I feel, however, that this is only because the visiting anglers had no plug baits. There are good shikaris to be had here who really know their work. They will on the whole advise against the plug, but other than this their advice is to be trusted. Apart from the Junction Pool the rest of the fishing is in the Poonch. With time to spare it is well worth while to fish up the Poonch river, particularly if snow water is coming down the Jhelum. Try junctions with the side streams ; the fish collect in such places. To mention one of them, the Bhan Nala junction. There is a large rock below the junction, and just below it there are always a few good fish.

Licences to fish Tangrot can be obtained from the Fisheries Jemadar on the spot for Rs. 3 per day. A boat with two men and the shikari costs a further Rs. 2-8 per diem.

There are two Bungalows : first the Government one with all amenities and four bedrooms. Secondly, the Kashmir State Forest Rest House with two bedrooms. In the latter case it is necessary to take with you all food and cooking arrangements. Permission must also be obtained from the State Authorities. It is by far the better situated of the two, and is so placed that a cool breeze may be enjoyed even on the hottest days. All drinking water must be boiled, and the water of the Poonch is preferable for this purpose to that of the Jhelum.

Snow water ceases to come down the Poonch on or about May 20th, which makes Tangrot a possibility for a week-end in the hot weather from such places as 'Pindi, Lahore, and Jhelum.   To get there, turn off the main Jhelum Wazirabad road where it crosses the Upper Jhelum Canal, and motor up the canal road to the canal headworks at Mangla (permit to use the road from Executive Engineer, Upper Jhelum Canal, Mangla). The road may not be used at night or during rain, and a speed limit of 30 m.p.h. is in force.   Before setting out on your trip, write to the Fisheries Jemadar at Tangrot, or to the Dak Bungalow Khansamah, and ask for a shikari to be sent to meet you at Mangla with such transport as you require (camels or pack ponies.)*   Then to Tangrot up the left bank of the river, where one crosses the river by the ferry to get to the Dak Bungalow.   For the return trip I strongly advise taking a boat from the Jhelum to Mangla (cost five rupees).   These boats are large and take four persons and their baggage easily.

Excellent sport may be had with Butchwa between the road and rail bridge at Jhelum at the top end of the Bazaar (right bank).   Butchwa are plentiful and apart from spinning tactics may be taken with bait in the following manner.   Whip two small hooks to a length of 2x gut.   The hooks should be nine inches apart and baited with congealed blood or soft liver.   Fish with a float from a boat, but strike quickly when the float disappears.

Sialkot District.   Good fishing may be had at Marala Weir, which is reached up the canal bank from the main Sialkot Wazirabad road.   Permission to use this road must be obtained from the Executive Engineer, Marala. There is a very pleasant Bungalow at Marala, which may be occupied with permission from the canal people.   It is necessary to take one's own servants and all stores, etc.   The fishing is best in the autumn, after the

* Hire of camel Rs. 2-8 ; and Rs. 1-8 per pony, plus baksheesh of course.   Camels are preferable as they don't bounce one's kit about so much.

Chenab river has cleared, and extends in a good year, when there has not been much rain, to as late as the end of December. Use a large plug or natural bait. Mahseer are to be had up to fifty pounds in weight and also some fine mulley nearly as large. The Chenab is peculiar in that the fish take best in the afternoon, the period between three o'clock and nightfall being the best. Fish both above and below the weir and where the Jammu Tawi joins the main stream. A glance at fig. 12, page 62. "A Typical Canal Headworks," gives the best stances for spinning at Marala. In the last fortnight of April and the first fortnight of May good sport may be had if the chilwa are running, before the snow water comes down.

A large country boat may be chartered, and, going upstream for about three miles, the Manawar junction may be fished, where the Bhimber Tawi joins the main stream. Then as far as Gangwal on the left bank there is nothing very much. About one and a half miles above Gangwal the river splits up into several branches, and at some of these junctions very good sport may be had. Care should be taken not to cross the Jammu border, which runs near here, unless a Jammu State fishing licence has been obtained. About four miles above Gangwal on the right bank, near the village of Nawanshahr, are some fine deep pools and runs under cliffs which hold large fish. The Bhimber Tawi is not affected by snow water, hence one's chances are fairly good at all times of the year, though in the hot weather the heat is far too great for comfortable fishing. This area is also somewhat malarious in the rains, at which time the fishing is at its worst too.

From Sialkot the Jammu Tawi may be fished. This is a really delightful stream to fish in October, November and December. A licence must be obtained from the Assistant Game Warden, Jammu State, Jammu, the cost of which is three rupees a day or thirty rupees for the year. The Tawi is a typical mahseer stream of the foothills, and, using a plug in clear water, good sport may be confidently expected. March and April are fair months for mahseer though not as good as the autumn. The Tawi may be fished from the sixth milestone from Jammu on the Kashmir road as far as Udhampur. The river between these two places is well off the beaten track, and though it may be fished by staying at Udhampur Dak Bungalow it is best to take camping equipment and, starting from Udhampur, fish downstream. There are a number of sacred pools which must be left alone, and two or three small stretches which are reserved for His Highness of Jammu and Kashmir.

Ambala District: Rupar. Here are the headworks of the Sirhind Canal which takes part of the waters of the Sutlej river. Rupar is best reached from the Grand Trunk Road. Turn left about 16 miles south of Ludhiana, where an excellent main canal road leads you direct to the three Rest Houses at Rupar Headworks. The canal headworks are a mile beyond the town. There are several bungalows here which may be occupied with permission of the Executive Engineer. The headworks are very much the same as given in the plan in Chapter IV, and the best places for fishing are as shewn. Use a smallish plug (the Pal-o'-Mine size 3 inches and Perch markings) and natural bait, as the fish do not run very large — the average ranging from three to ten pounds, though an occasional fish of twenty pounds is taken. The months of April and May are very good, and the fishing is at its best in hot, calm, dry, settled weather. The threadline with natural bait may be used successfully when the chilwa are running.

The main river can be fished with some success for a distance of some four hundred yards below the weir, and with the aid of a local boat some good stretches may be reached a few miles above the headworks. Rupar is a very pretty place and makes a delightful short trip before the hot weather sets in.

Jullundur District : The Lower Beas. This is an excellent bit of water and, to my mind, probably the best on offer for large fish in the whole of the Beas. Of a number of good stretches, the best are Rora and Pant pools.

The most-convenient base for operations is Talwara Dak Bungalow, which is reached by a bad road from Makerian, which in turn may be got at by rail from Jullundur or by road from Gurdaspur. Talwara may also be reached from Hoshiarpur by a vile road. From Talwara there is another wretched track which is just motorable to Rora ferry, where there is a fine run with a grand pool below it. The baits *par excellence* are a large quiet-coloured plug, the natural chilwa, or a small mahseer, spun slowly. A prawn in the tail of the stream is also a bait not to be despised.

By crossing the river and camping at Pant some two miles further on, Pant Pool and another large pool and run above it may be fished. Fish of seventy pounds have been taken here, and I believe the hundred pounder is to be had in time.

The best periods for fishing in this stretch of water are the months of March and April and then again in October and November.

There is also good fishing to be had at Dehra Gopipur, which is to be reached from Hoshiarpur by a poor road. From Dehra Gopipur one may fish up the Beas, finding good runs and pools nearly all the way to Mandi and beyond. The higher up the river one goes, lighter-coloured plugs are more killing, and unjointed models take pride of place.

To write fully of all the good localities in the Beas would fill volumes ; it is by far the best fishing river in the Punjab, and is by no means inaccessible if one is prepared to work for one's fishing. Information, and the licences necessary, are always to be had for the asking from the office of the Game Warden, Lahore.

Kangra and the Middle Beas. There are quite a fair number of good fishing streams in the Kangra district which are tributaries of the Beas River. They are locally known as Khads. The lowest few miles of these Khads and their junction with the main Beas River should always receive the careful attention of the angler, as fish tend to congregate in such places at all times of the year. On the main river itself the best stretches are as follows (starting from Talwara and going upstream) :—

Simbal, Nurwaneh, Dehra Gopipur (bungalow), Kalesar, Nadaun (bungalow), Sujanpur (bungalow), Ambragaon, and finally Mandi itself. The junction of the Rana Khad with the Beas is another good spot. This is the stream which comes down from Jogindernagar on the Baijnath-Mandi road. From Rana Khad junction up to Mandi the river is not easily approached nor is the water too good for light fishing.

There is a stream which flows below the Dak Bungalow at Baijnath-Paprola (a good halting place for the night when motoring up to Kulu) and eventually joins the Beas. From this junction downstream the Beas is more open and approachable. The Baijnath stream itself holds some very nice mahseer, and I have had some pleasant days of fishing when staying at Baijnath Bungalow, using the threadline and trout tackle. It is a typical mountain mahseer stream, and in the lower few miles holds some large fish.

The Ravi River. A good mahseer river, but little fished in its upper reaches owing to its inaccessibility. It may be reached from Dalhousie by a hill track to a place called Simbalau, where good fishing may be had at the junction of the main river and a tributary. From her it is just possible for the very fit to follow the river down to Madhopur by using the hill tracks. But even so it is by no means possible to fish all the way down, as in many places the river cannot be reached. When approaching the Ravi from Dalhousie care should be taken not to cross over and fish in Chamba State territory, as the boundary runs near Simbalau.

The easier way of fishing the Ravi is to start where it emerges from the hills and work upwards until one comes to a dead stop.

From Pathankote, which is on both the main road and the railway, Madhopur may be reached, eight miles distant, where there is a canal headworks. When there is enough water there are plenty of good mahseer above the weir for a distance of two or three miles, some of them running to as much as thirty pounds in weight. The chief factor which militates against Madhopur Weir for fishing is a frequent lack of water From Madhopur upstream the right bank of the Rawi is in Jammu State territory.

From Pathankote, Shahpur and Basaoli may be reached, both places offering excellent mahseer water.

The Upper Beas. At Mandi the Sukheti stream joins the Beas. Skene Dhu reports the stream to be completely ruined. It must have recovered a lot since he wrote of it, as thirty-pounders are to be seen both above and below the town, and at the junction near the bridge. Here the Beas River and its side streams are in Mandi State, and a mahseer fishing licence must be obtained from the Chief Revenue Officer. The fees for fishing are not high, being Rs. 2 for two days, Rs. 5 for ten days or less, and Rs. 10 for a month. Enquiries should be made in Mandi as some of the streams are charged for separately. Mandi State is very anxious to improve its fishing and sport obtainable, and everything possible is done to help the visitor.

Above Mandi mahseer are known to run up as far as the Parbati junction, and are usually to be found at the Sainj and Tirthan junctions. From a little below Larji down to the Suspension Brdige at Pandoh, the Beas runs through a terifying gorge, where fishing is very difficult. At Pandoh, just above the Suspension Bridge, the Juni Khad joins the river. The junction at Pandoh holds some very large fish. There is a most excellent bungalow here, permission to occupy which may be had from the Sub-Divisional Officer, P.W.D., Kulu.

Excellent fishing is to be had in the Juni Khad, which consists of large deep pools and connecting channels for a distance of fully four miles above Pandoh Bungalow. The pools above and below the Suspension Bridge (about a mile up the Juni from Pandoh) hold fish up to thirty pounds to my certain knowledge.

There is another fine little mahseer stream, the Bakhli Khad which can be reached from Pandoh. The junction is four miles up the left bank of the Beas by a forest track. Though not as good as the Juni Khad there are some nice pools near the Suspension Bridge, a little way up from the junction, which hold fish of about the fifteen-pound mark.

Ten days spent fishing the Sukheti from Mandi and the two Khads mentioned above from Pandoh would repay one well in the last fortnight of September or beginning of October.

The Simla Hills. The fullest details of the fishing to be had in this area are given in *The Angler in Northern India*. Conditions have not changed much since, and the intending fisherman cannot do better than to study this book before embarking on an expedition. The following notes are given in amplification, and for those who have not a copy of Skene Dhu's book by them.

The two main fishing rivers south of Simla are the Giri and the Gamber. Fishing in the Giri starts at Khargaon, a village about a mile above the junction of the Ashni (or Simla Stream) and the Giri. From this point to its junction with the Jumna, a distance of some seventy miles, the stream runs through Sirmoor State. Fishing permits are to be had on application to the Foreign and Political Minister, Sirmoor State, Nahan. The fees are thirty rupees for the season or two rupees per day for each rod. Mahseer and an occasional goonch are the only fish on offer.

If the winter rains have been good the spring fishing is very good ; September, October, and the first weeks of November are always excellent. The reach of the river from Khargaon to a place called Majere, a distance of six miles, is convenient to fish on a week-end. The shortest way to get to Khargaon is to take one's car to a point immediately below Salogra Station, which is about three miles beyond Solon on the Kalka Simla Road. From here a rideable path leads down to the bed of the Ashni, which should

Plate XII   SPRING IN THE HILLS

be followed to the junction, the total distance from the motor road being about seven miles. Fish from two to twenty pounds may be had on this stretch, and the fishing continues to improve both as regards size of fish and general quality the whole way down to the junction of the Giri with the Jumna.

If your fishing trip is of long duration and you intend to fish beyond Majere, a tent and all supplies are necessary, as apart from small bunnias shops, where food can be got for the porters, nothing is to be had, fowls, milk and vegetables not being exceptions.

The Gamber is a delightful little stream and is ideal for the threadline. The easiest way to get there is *via* Subathu. Except during a break in the rains, when fish up to five pounds may be had at Kakarhalli (three miles below Subathu on the old Kalka Simla bridle-path), the fishing does not commence till one reaches Bagaruhatti, which is ten miles down stream from Kakarhalli, i.e., thirteen miles from Subathu. Excellent sport may be had with fish up to ten pounds in weight at a point five miles below Bagaruhatti in September and October.

The river runs through half-dozen or more small states, starting with Mahlog and ending with Nalagarh. These states auction the fishing rights to local fishermen, and the stream is badly netted. But in spite of this good fishing is to be had after the rains. Here again, the spring fishing depends on whether the winter rains have been good.

From Bagaruhatti there is thirty miles of very good fishing down to the junction of the stream with the Sutlej. This may be fished both in the spring and in the autumn. Permission should be obtained through the Political Officer, Simla Hill States, though local permission is always to be had by giving the fisherman who has the rights a couple of rupees. No supplies whatever are available. It is a great pity that this river is not preserved, as it has really strong runs and the maximum sport is had with the lightest of fish.

In the upper reaches of both the Giri and the Gamber the threadline and a baby devon minnow, or the mother-of-pearl bar spoon, stands by itself. The two hook lure, with or without the spinning head, may also be used with execution if one is satisfied with more modest sizes of fish. As one gets further down stream the short rod and the plug are more suitable.

Delhi District. Okhla (the Jumna) is within twenty minutes of Delhi by car, yet is very little fished by those stationed in Delhi. It is a very pleasant spot for a picnic, and I am sure holds very fair fishing possibilities. The local natives get quite a few fish but not many mahseer. The best time is in March when the chilwa are running. Large goonch and mulley have been taken here with spinning tackle. The Okhla is typical of plains fishing and does not really come within the province of this book. I have only mentioned it as a possibility for those who wish to keep their hand in and cannot get away to better waters.

The Punjab : United Provinces Border. Under this heading I refer to the Jumna from the Giri junction down to Tajuwala and Hathnikand, a very pleasant stretch of water which offers chances of using both the threadline and the short rod. The best times for this river are March and again in October. After April 1st, snow water is likely to come down and spoil the sport. The Asan Junction and a mile or two on the left bank is preserved by the Dehra Dun Fishing Association. Below the junction there is about ten miles of good water till Khara is reached. Here there is an Irrigation Bungalow, to occupy which permission must be obtained from the Executive Engineer, Western Jumna Canal, Saharanpur. Khara may be reached by car from Saharanpur. Between Khara and the Asan Junction there are two pools of special note, Pounta Pool and the Fakirs' Pool.

Tajuwala and Hathnikand are on the opposite bank and about four to six miles down stream from Khara, and are reached from the Delhi Saharanpur road by motoring up the canal bank from Jagadhri. There is a canal bungalow at Tajuwala (Western Jumna Canal), and a forest rest house at Hathnikand, to occupay which permission must be obtained beforehand.

The peculiar attraction of the Jumna is that the river splits up into a number of separate channels in many places, so that one may change from the threadline to heavier tackle and back again as the occasion warrants.

The most popular baits are plugs of all kinds and the natural fish spun slowly. Threadline devon minnows and a mother-of-pearl bar spoon are also good in places.

Trout Fishing in Kulu. The Kulu Valley is best reached *via* Pathankot by car. The motor road for a distance of about 100 miles (through Mandi State and the Kulu district) is bad ; but by careful driving, and careful attention to one's car before the start, the journey can be accomplished without mishap. Fortunately, the best fishing periods are those in which least trouble may be expected on the road. During the monsoon months (June, July, August) the journey is somewhat of a hazardous undertaking and the rivers are also in full flood.

The season is a long one, extending from March till October. The month of April and the last fortnight of September and the first fortnight of October are probably the best periods for the bigger fish. The waters are stocked with Brown trout and Rainbow. The former, however, represent most of the bag. The size limit for trout is ten inches and the angler is limited to eight fish a day on a single licence, and twelve on a "family licence." The "family licence" includes a man, his wife and his children in any combination of two. Before going to Kulu it is best to refer to the latest rules in force, as the Game Warden, Punjab, has the power to alter rules governing licences, size, and numbers of fish to be taken, at the beginning of each fishing season.

Personally I was not fortunate enough to take a fish over two and a half pounds in weight, but every year fish of well over this weight are killed, the largest fish of last season (1938) being a Brown trout of ten pounds netted at the junction of the Sainj and Tirthan rivers. Another of six pounds was taken by an angler just below Kulu town, on the humble worm.

Unlike Kashmir, the river is not divided into beats. The visiting angler therefore has a vast mileage of water to choose from. Provision exists, however, for the division of the river into beats when there is any danger of overcrowding.

The angler is allowed to use fly, spinning bait (artificial or natural), and worm on the main Beas river. In the side streams the worm is not permitted. The cost of a licence to cover *all* trout waters in the district is Rs. 25 per month for the single angler, or thirty rupees to include his wife as well.

The main Beas River and the side streams running into it from just above Kulu town (Sultanpur) to source constitute the "Angling Reserve." Above Manali very little sport may be expected, as the water is normally too cold. Into the Beas run the Sujjain, Phojal, Chakki and Chirid streams. In the main river there are excellent long deep pools which contain some remarkable fish. They are, however, sometimes difficult of access, as the water is fast and often entails a good deal of wading. The side streams offer the best sport, particularly the Phojal and Sujjain nalas. They are on an average some dozen yards in width and remind one of the streams of Yorkshire and Scotland. The water should be gin clear for the best results, and the fish are very bold takers. In the early part of the year the main river contains nearly all the fish, but as soon as the water warms up the fish move up the side streams. The hanks of these side streams are much overgrown, with the result that the services of a local shikari are desirable in order to save loss of tackle (pay Rs. 15 per month).

Below Kulu town the main river is netted by local natives which detracts from its popularity with visiting sportsmen. The Sarbarri river joins the Beas here also. This stream used to offer the best trouting in the valley, until netting was permitted. The Sarbarri is the best natural spawning stream in Kulu and has again been closed to netsmen this year, so that hopes of excellent sport may be entertained for the future.

The visiting sportsman may fish any of the above streams whilst residing, as I did, "at mine ease in mine inn," but for the rivers mentioned hereafter camping is necessary.

Some seven miles below Kulu on the right bank the Parbati river joins the Beas. This river has been regularly stocked for years, and, with the exception of the occasional forest officer or local native, is never fished. The licence is ridiculously cheap, costing but a few rupees. The fishing is magnificent, but the sportsman must take full camp equipment and supplies, Furthermore, a good servant is essential, as the natives who inhabit this area – and, for that matter, the whole valley – are as indolent, dirty, unhelpful and disobliging a crowd as one could wish to avoid the world over.

About 25 miles below Kulu, on the same bank, are the Sainj and Tirthan rivers. Again the rod licence for these rivers costs about five rupees per month. The fishing is also excellent, but owing to their low altitude they are best fished in spring and autumn. The Sainj river joins the Tirthan near Larji. The upper reaches are well off the beaten track, and camping is necessary. There is a Forest Rest House at Sainj, for which permission may be obtained to occupy from the Divisional Forest Officer, Seraj Forest Division, Kulu, Kangra District.

The Tirthan is a first-class fishing river. The best fishing is from Bali (Mandi Police Post) six miles upstream from Larji to Banjar and Bandal. Good trout may be taken from the pools forming the heads of mill channels at Bali. From Larji to Manglour the left bank is Mandi State territory and the right bank British India. There are rest houses at Larji and Banjar which may be occupied. The river lies across the pack road from Kulu to Simla, and forms an interesting and pleasant trek from the latter resort. This trip was given some publicity two years ago, as H. E. The Viceroy paid a visit to the Kulu Sub-Division for the fishing.

The prospect of fishing in future years is very favourable. A hatchery exists at Katrain and another is shortly to be opened. Research work on the food supply and insect life on the trout waters has also been taken in hand.

Licences may be had from the Fisheries Jemadar at Katrain or from Tysonia Hotel. Intending fishermen are advised to obtain their licences on the spot, as fees are not returnable. A report of the size and numbers of fish taken must be made on the reverse of the licence, which has to be returned on its expiry.

Trout Fishing in Mandi State. Very good trouting may now be had by the visiting fisherman in the Uhl River in Mandi State. A few years ago these waters were practically ruined by dynamiting, but the State authorities have now taken matters in hand, and recent reports go to prove that the trouting is rapidly recovering and will soon bid fair to rival the Kulu Streams. Mandi is an Indian state and lies across the road from Pathankote to Kulu. Licences for trout fishing are to be had from the Revenue Secretary, Mandi Darbar. For a period up to ten days the charge is fifteen rupees, and for a month forty-five rupees per rod. These fees should by now have been reduced to those ruling in the Kangra District, as this was part of the agreement made by the Game Warden and entered into with Mandi State when the Uhl River was restocked.

Last year 6,000 rainbow trout ova were planted and are reported to be progressing favourably. Owing to the fact that the Uhl runs through some very deep gorges where fishing is quite out of the question, there should never be a dearth of good sized fish, as these un-get-at-able reaches afford natural sanctuaries. The river runs through magnificent scenery and is remarkable for the clearness of its waters and for the beautiful coloured stones in its bed.

There are three main localities for trout fishing. The first is a place called Kamand which is reached by bridle path from Mandi town, a distance of ten miles. As there is no rest house or dak bungalow here all kit and stores must be taken on pack transport. There is, however, a rest house four miles from Kamand at Kataula, permission to use which must be obtained from the State Authorities. The second is at Jhatingri, which is reached by a bridle path three miles from the motor road between Joginder-nagar and Urla Ghoma Cross. Here there is a small bazaar where supplies such as potatoes, eggs, and milk may be obtained ; the fishing is about two miles from Jhatingri. The third locality is in the vicinity of Brot, where is situated the headworks of the Punjab Hydro Electric Department. There is a rest house here which may be occupied with permission of the Resident Engineer, Jogindernagar, Mandi State. Brot may be reached either by foot on a very steep mountain path from Jogindernagar, a distance of some ten miles (and very hard going), or by going up in a truck on the Hydro Electric haulage way, for which permission must be obtained and an indemnity bond executed.

For anyone with a month to spend in spring or autumn I would suggest going to Jogindernagar by rail and thence to Mandi by motor-bus. Stop a night at Mandi in the palatial dak bungalow and fix up some transport arrangements, then make for Kamand and fish upstream to Brot. Alternatively, one might take a car to Jogindernagar and garage it there, and then going up to Brot, fish downstream to Kamand, returning from Mandi by bus to Jogindernagar.

The licence for this river is very generous in its terms, and allows the fisherman a wider choice of baits and lures : artificial fly, natural fly, artificial and natural minnow, and worm being allowed. Thus the angler may use the clear water worm in ideal conditions, and the fish taken with this method lave nothing to be desired as regards size.

The season is a long one and extends from March 1st to the last day of October. The size limit for trout is twelve inches, and the limit for numbers for a ten-day licence is thirty fish, and one hundred for the monthly ticket.

Threadline is the ideal tackle for the River Uhl, though the short rod should be taken for the mahseer fishing, which is very good in Mandi State and which is described in the section dealing with the Upper Beas and Kangra.

No one who is not 100 per cent. fit should attempt to fish the Uhl, as the going is very hard and entails a great deal of climbing. The months of July and August should be avoided as the rains come down with a ferocity which must be experienced to be believed. I was once caught in this area when on my way to Kulu ; some eight and half inches of rain fell in a single night, washing away miles of road and nineteen bridges, not to mention the fact that an entire village was swept away in a landslide, not even a single goat or fowl srviving !

Trout Fishing in Kangra. Though easily reached in a day from Lahore or Jullundur in a car, surprisingly few people know of the trouting to be had in Kangra in the Baner River at Dadh. There is a Civil Rest House at Dadh which may be occupied with permission, and it is reached by a good road all the way. To get there, motor to Pathankot and thence take the road to Palampur and Kulu : turn left off the main road two miles beyond Nargrota, and follow this road to its end. This is only a fair weather road. The trout fishing is about four miles up the hill from the Bungalow. It is rather a doubtful quantity as a trout stream, for one may go there one day and have quite fair sport, and yet on another occasion not touch a fish. It is, however, a very pleasant trip for a short leave and well worth making.

Permits to fish are obtained from the Inspector of Fisheries, Palampur. The intention, if not the rule, is that fly and spinning only are allowed. A good time to go would be at Easter, when the weather is delightful and the combing from the Bungalow to the stream would not be found over strenuous.

The Baner river has not proved a great success as a trout river, owing to the extremely heavy spates which occur in the rains and which wash the fish away into the main river. I also feel that a great deal of quiet poaching goes on, as the local Dogras are very fond of fish and make the most of the trout put there by a kind Government for their delectation. They are withal a much more go-ahead race than the inhabitants of the Kulu valley, who are entirely apathetic to the presence of trout and resent the instrusion of the fisherman, or anyone else for that matter.

There is one other trout stream, the Gaj River, but like the Baner it has proved very difficult to stock. Something like 200,000 trout ova have been planted in the last twenty years, and all that is to be had is a sprinkling of very large fish but no fry or yearlings. In its present state it hardly warrants a visit.

Trout Fishing in the Simla Hills. Bashahr State, the largest of the many Simla Hill States, has two trout streams, the Pabar and the Baspa. The former joins the Tons River lower down, whilst the Baspa flows direct to the Sutlej. Neither of them is easy to get at, and entails complete camping arrangements. A visit to the Baspa would require twelve days' marching from Simla along the Hindustan-Thibet road. The Baspa is a truly magnificent stream which flows through quite the loveliest valley in the Himalayas. The trout are big and as fat as butter, and rise readily to the "fly lure." Information on the Baspa may be had from the Divisional Forest Officer, Upper Bashahr Division, Phillaur.

The Pabar is also good and information regarding it may be had for the asking from the Divisional Forest Officer, Lower Bashahr Division, Kotgarh.

Trout Fishing in the Kagan Valley (N.W.F.P.) Though the Kagan lies outside the Political Boundary of the Punjab, I feel that its inclusion in this list of trouting localities is warranted on account of its being so easily reached from Peshawar, Rawalpindi and Jhelum. This part of the world is really very accessible, wholly delightful and yet very little known, and gives an opportunity to anyone anxious to spend a cheap fishing leave in the hills and avoid the flesh-pots of Kashmir.

To get there, motor to Abbottabad and on to Mansehra on the Kashmir road, turn left off the main road just short of Gahri Habibullah and thence to Balakote. At Balakote make arrangements to garage one's car and transfer stores and kit to pack transport. There is a Bungalow here where one may stay and make the necessary arrangements for the mules. From Balakote one must march or ride to Naran in the Kagan valley for the trout fishing. The marches are Balakote–Bela Kawai, 13 miles ; thence to Mahander 14 miles, thence to Kagan 12 miles, and finally from Kagan to Naran 14 miles. There are P.W.D. Rest Houses at Bela Kawai, Mahander, Kagan and Naran. Permission to use them is readily given by the Superintending Engineer or the P.W.D. at Abbottabad, but it is advisable to take a tent in case of emergencies.

Licences are granted free by the Conservator of Forests, N.W.F.P., Abbottabad, to a limited number of approved rods in the year. The fishing is not officially open yet. Where, however, a licence to fish is given, the following conditions are imposed :—

(i) That the fish not required by the permit holder are returned to the river.

(ii) That the permit holder furnishes a complete note on the fishing at the end of his tour.

At Naran the river opens out and offers the nearest thing to perfection for threadline spinning I know. A friend of mine reported that the largest fish he took weighed a full four pounds, and that he cannot remember ever

MORNING CATCH
Kulu 1938.

Plate XIII   BAGAIRNAM RIVER

having landed a fish of under a pound in weight! He was using the threadline and the baby devon minnow.

The best months for fishing are from July to September immediately after the rush of water consequent on the thawing of the snow in the hills has subsided. October may be equally good, but it is too cold to go up the valley then with any degree of comfort. The valley is fortunate in being outside the influence of the monsoonic rains, though during the months of July and August one may reckon on having one wet day in three. It is possible that the fishing might also be good in April, but I can get no report from anyone ever having been there during this month.

The Kagan in time to come should offer some very good sport to those stationed in the northern Punjab and the North West Frontier Province. Fortunately, the local people higher up the valley do not like fish and therefore don't attempt to poach, which seems very nearly too good to be true. The trout appear to inhabit only some sixteen miles of water, seven miles above Naran and nine miles below. Though there is perfect water higher up at altitudes in which trout flourish in Kashmir, the Kagan Brown trout do not appear either to thrive there, or, alternatively, to have worked their way up there yet. Personally I am of the opinion that the latter alternative is the most likely.

Trout Fishing in Kashmir. Though outside the geographical and political limits of this book, Kashmir trout-fishing is so much the goal of the angler in India that to omit reference thereto would make this little book sadly incomplete.

To attempt a full description of all the trout waters of this delightful country in the short compass of a few pages is an impossible task. Furthermore, the State Authorities can and will supply much information to the intending visitor if approached. In spite of this, however, there is a real call for a good book on Kashmir trouting. There must be many residents who have the requisite knowledge, and were one of them to write a fully descriptive book I feel confident that, not only would he receive the plaudits of fishermen and the State authorities, but would also be sure of a good sale for his labours.

The trout fishing in Kashmir is all State-controlled ; in fact, nowadays it might almost be termed an industry. Kashmir caters for the tourist above all else, hence the costs for a fishing trip are considerably higher than in British India. Here the trout waters are divided into beats, which must be booked in advance. To obtain the best from one's fishing it is necessary to book a long time ahead, and to make careful arrangements regarding the dates of one's leave. For if at the last moment it is impossible to go, the licence fees are not returnable although sub-letting of the fishings taken can often be arranged.

The trout waters may be classified roughly as follows :—

The Bringhi Valley	8 beats.
The Sind Valley	6 beats.
The Madmati, Erin, and Gurais Valleys	4 beats.
The Liddar Valley	3 beats.

Over and above these are the lakes and such new waters as the Kotsu stream, of which I do not propose to treat. Most of the beats carry two rods apiece. When planning a fishing trip it is essential that proper regard be paid to the time of year, for some waters are at their best early and others late, and are in certain circumstances altogether unfishable owing to snow water and timber. Detailed information regarding these matters is given in the pamphlet supplied by the Game Warden, Srinagar, which may be had on application.

In April, May and June the lower beats on the Bringhi offer good sport. The Nowboog upper and lower are very good and come into their own from May onwards. The Kokarnag in the Bringhi area is a spring-fed stream and is consequently unaffected by snow water. It offers extremely good trouting, but can only be had for two days at a time as there is great competition for rods. The Desu, another stream in the Bringhi area, is best fished from June onwards.

The Sind valley waters are both early and very late. Probably the month of April and the first few days of May, and then again the last days of August and the whole of September are best. The beat in the lowest stretch of the Sind is a daily water and may be fished from Srinagar.

The fishing in the Gurais valley consists of the Burdwan stream and the Kishenganga river. The former is a small stream, and though abounding in trout seldom rewards the angler with anything over a pound in weight. The Kishenganga holds some very fine fish, but much trouble is experienced with snow water, when it becomes a raging torrent. It does, however, clear late in the year and good sport may be had in the last week of August and the whole of September. The Burdwan stream is spring-fed and is fishable throughout the season.

The Madmati is a good stream and may be fished throughout the year. It covers a large area and offers a great variety to the fisherman. The Erin Nala is the same. This is a truly beautiful stream, and the scenery absolutely beggars description.

Finally we have the Liddar, which is divided into the Aru and the Shishnag. Of the two, the last named is probably the better. August and September are the best months for this area. The water is often spoilt for the fisherman by bathers and pilgrims – truly a case of "where only man is vile !"

For all Kashmir trout fishing the fisherman must saddle himself with a shikari – a great imposition, as his pay is thirty rupees a month plus the inevitable baksheesh. Licence fees are also very high when compared to the very moderate fees which a fisherman has to pay in Kulu. Kashmir, is, however, a country for the rich man and tourist from afar, so it is not very surprising.

Threadline is *the* tackle for all Kashmir waters ; where spinning is allowed it is in a class by itself, and in fly only waters the leaded lure, with or without the spinning head, kills well. The short rod may also be used with the smallest size of plugs ; for patterns the smallest size of Pal-o'-Mine (perch markings) and some of the "Hardy-Jock Scott Wigglers" are good.

Many fishermen will wish to combine trekking with their fishing. This forms a truly delightful holiday and one during which there should never be a regrettable day. I have the following suggested itinerary in my notes. It was given me by a man I met in the Rawalpindi Club bar. As I cannot remember his name I am unfortunately unable to give him my acknowledgements and thanks for the information.

Starting on August 1st from Srinagar, trek up the Erin valley and fish therein for a week ; thence move to the Madmati for a further week's fishing. After that move to Gurais *via* Tragbal and Koraghbal to Kamri, where there is a very pretty rest house. From here go to the top of the pass for a view of Nanga Parbat. From Kamri move camp to Burdwan, and fish the Burdwan stream and the Kishenganga for the first part of September. The trek from the Madmati to the Kishenganga area will in itself take about a week or ten days, if done slowly and enjoying the magnificent scenery the surroundings have to offer. Finally trek back to Srinagar *via* Koraghbal, Tragbal and Bandipura, where a lorry may be engaged for the last lap to Srinagar. Such a trip, with a few days spent at Srinagar making the necessary arrangements before the start, and a further few days at the end, will just about occupy a two-months' leave. Odd days may be spent in trying for choosh, chirro and snow trout. The cost should not prove prohibitive, and if you are a family man the family will not find the going too hard.

The Fishing Register. I must strongly advise any fisherman to keep up a fishing register. Apart from forming a pleasant reminder of happy days, it is an invaluable aid to successful fishing. If kept up in some detail, a fishing diary will in a very short time give anyone sufficient data to base the choice of a bait or lure, and on which to decide when to go and where to fish. A suggested specimen page is shewn overleaf. Such pages may be ruled out on drawing paper and stuck into a large photograph album, with say a blank page here and there on which may be pasted such photographs as you may collect. It is amazing how in a very short while it is possible to collect such a mine of information and personal observation, that it is more valuable by far than any printed book which money can buy.

Another piece of advice which was given me, and which I have never regretted following, is the keeping of a locality register as well. Nearly every week one hears of some river or stream or place where good fishing is to be had. All too frequently it is soon forgotten and even the name of the man who spoke of it. If such knowledge is noted down in a notebook, as in the case of the fishing register, in a short while a great deal of invaluable information may be collected. That it may not be of use to you today is nothing ; you never know where you will be stationed at some future date. And, believe me, it is very gratifying to find on arrival in a new station that you have something to start with.

In days past I should have now said "I lay down my pen thankful that I have been permitted to bring this work to a close." Actually, I have knocked hell out of my typewriter, and it is about time the poor thing had a rest. That I have enjoyed it I won't deny.

I hope most sincerely that the information given in the preceding pages will enable you to get better fishing. If it does my satisfaction is complete.

LOCALITY	FISH	WEIGHT OR MEASUREMENTS	BAIT	REMARKS (Date, Weather Conditions, etc.)
K U L U Sujjain Nala	Trout	2½ lbs., 21 lbs. 1 lb. 6 ozs. 1¼ lbs., 1 lb.	Natural minnow in a Scarab Mounting	September 9th 1937. Taken in the big pool under the falls at the top of the nala. Very fast clear water. Time 9-30 to 11 a.m. Clear blue sky, warm light wind. Returned three fish under the limit.
Beas River (Naggar Bridge)	Trout Barbel	1 lb. 14 ozs. 12 ozs. 4½ lbs.	Worm	All taken below the bridge, 3 trouts put back. Time 5 to 6 p.m. Showery.

LOCALITY	FISH	REMARKS
P U N J A B Sialkot District **CHENAB RIVER** Marala Canal Head-works	Mahseer Mulley Goonch	Reached by canal road from Sialkot-Wazirabad main road. Canal pass to be had for use of road from Executive Engineer, Marala. (Telegraphic address X.E.N., Marala). Canal Bungalow—no supplies worth mentioning—permission to occupy from X.E.N. Best time for fishing is in the afternoon at all times of the year. The fishing is good in the spring and in the autumn, when the water is fairly clear and the weather settled. Licence to be had from Canal Office, Marala—8 annas per day or ten rupees per annum. **Later Note**—Major Ata Xerxes reports killing three fish. 25 lbs. and 12 lbs. (mahseer) and one mulley 9½ lbs. on May 2nd 1939.

STANDARD SCALE OF HOOK SIZES

By courtesy of

Messrs. Gogswell & Harrison Ltd.

168 Piccadilly W.I.

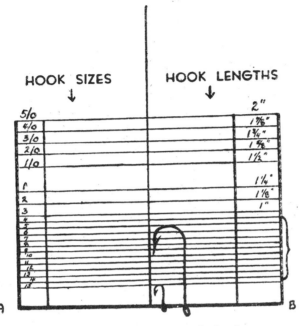

HOOK SIZES ↓　　**HOOK LENGTHS** ↓

Each size decreases by 1/16″ i.e. No. 4 is 15/16″—No. 5 is 14/16″ and so on.

Measure hooks as shewn above. Do not include the eye of the hook, which should be *just* below the line A—B. Hooks sizes 5 and 15 are shewn as examples—

OLD SCALE	15	14	13	12	11	10	9	8	7	6	5	4	3
NEW SCALE	0	1	2	3	4	5	6	7	8	9	10	11	12

As some tackleists use the old system of numbering and some the new system, the above conversion table is given. The actual sizes of the hooks are the same in either case.

Example :—No. 13 size hook "Old Scale" is the same as No. 2 new scale (i.e.,6/16″ in length).

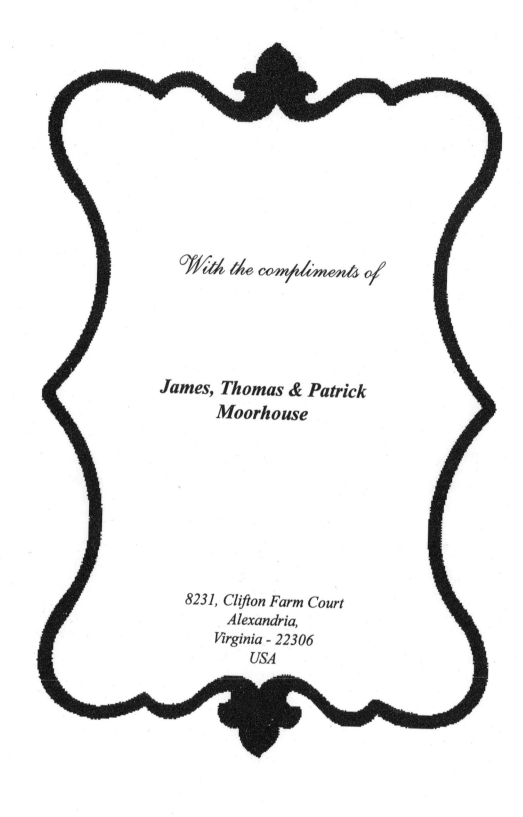

With the compliments of

**James, Thomas & Patrick
Moorhouse**

*8231, Clifton Farm Court
Alexandria,
Virginia - 22306
USA*

GABRIEL

DANA

Valeo

Henkel

Haldex

Purolator

Excellence in manufacturing.
World-class quality and services. Leadership
in technology. That's what attracted
the world's best names to us!
At the Anand Group, we believe in setting global
standards in the automotive component segment.
And our continued market leadership bears testimony
to our commitment and growth.
But the way we conduct our business is where our
real strength lies. Absorbing new technologies,
empowering people, applying innovative production
methods and a tradition of values.
All going into the making of a true leader.

THIS IS
HOW WORLD LEADERS
SEE US!

1

ANAND »
Our way is working.

ARVIN
EXHAUST

FEDERAL
MOGUL

Chang Yun

KYB

MANDO

FARR

BEHR

YAMAHA

Degrémont

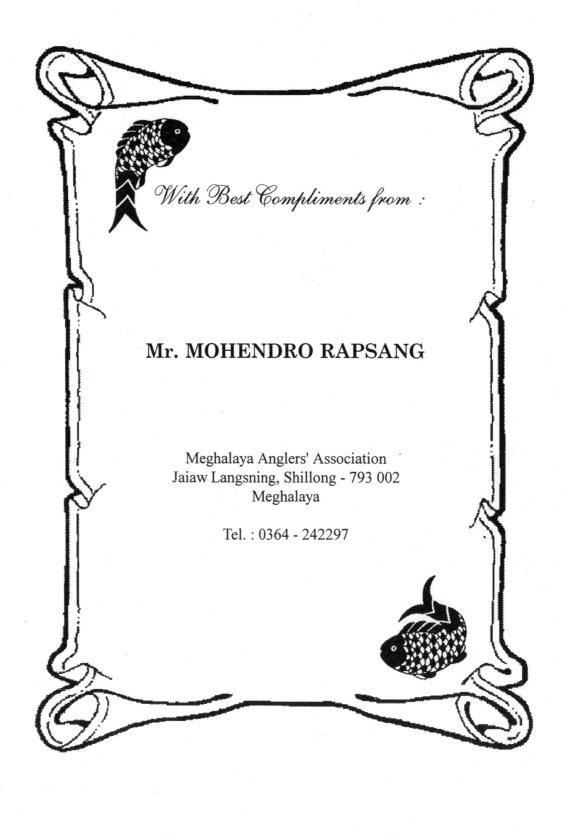

With Best Compliments from :

Mr. MOHENDRO RAPSANG

Meghalaya Anglers' Association
Jaiaw Langsning, Shillong - 793 002
Meghalaya

Tel. : 0364 - 242297

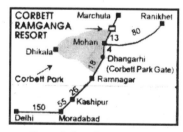

ESCORTS

Escorts is among the leading Indian Corporates with a significant presence in the business spheres of agri machinery, bi-wheelers, construction and material handling equipment, auto components, telecom and finance.

We believe that the value of a company and its prospects depend on the extent to which it can consolidate specialisation and enhance skills. Thus, business must be market driven, possess a realistic understanding of consumers' requirements and create value-added products through world class technology.

Adhering to the philosophy of core management, core business and core success, Escorts is all set to enter the next millennium as a global major.

Corporate Centre: 15/5 Mathura Road, Faridabad - 121 003, India. Tel: 0129 - 275981. Telefax: 0129 - 276728